REGENTS RESTORATION DRAMA SERIES

General Editor: John Loftis

THE ROVER

APHRA BEHN

The Rover

Edited by

FREDERICK M. LINK

UNIVERSITY OF NEBRASKA PRESS
LINCOLN AND LONDON

Regents Restoration Drama Series

The Regents Restoration Drama Series, similar in objectives and format to the Regents Renaissance Drama Series, will provide soundly edited texts, in modern spelling, of the more significant English plays of the late seventeenth and early eighteenth centuries. The word "Restoration" is here used ambiguously and must be explained. If to the historian it refers to the period between 1660 and 1685 (or 1688), it has long been used by the student of drama in default of a more precise word to refer to plays belonging to the dramatic tradition established in the 1660's, weakening after 1700, and displaced in the 1730's. It is in this extended sense—imprecise though justified by academic custom—that the word is used in this series, which will include plays first produced between 1660 and 1737. Although these limiting dates are determined by political events, the return of Charles II (and the removal of prohibitions against the operation of theaters) and the passage of Walpole's Stage Licensing Act, they enclose a period of dramatic history having a coherence of its own in the establishment, development, and disintegration of a tradition.

Each text in the series is based on a fresh collation of the seventeenth- and eighteenth-century editions that might be presumed to have authority. The textual notes, which appear above the rule at the bottom of each page, record all substantive departures from the edition used as the copy-text. Variant substantive readings among contemporary editions are listed there as well. Editions later than the eighteenth century are referred to in the textual notes only when an emendation originating in some one of them is received into the text. Variants of accidentals (spelling, punctuation, capitalization) are not recorded in the notes. Contracted forms of characters' names are silently expanded in speech prefixes and stage directions, and, in the case of speech prefixes, are regularized. Additions to the stage directions of the copy-text are enclosed in brackets. Stage directions such as "within" or "aside" are enclosed in parentheses when they occur in the copy-text.

Spelling has been modernized along consciously conservative lines, but within the limits of a modernized text the linguistic quality of the original has been carefully preserved. Contracted preterites have regularly been expanded. Punctuation has been brought into accord with modern practices. The objective has been to achieve a balance between the pointing of the old editions and a system of punctuation which, without overloading the text with exclamation marks, semicolons, and dashes, will make the often loosely flowing verse and prose of the original syntactically intelligible to the modern reader. Dashes are regularly used only to indicate interrupted speeches, or shifts of address within a single speech.

Explanatory notes, chiefly concerned with glossing obsolete words and phrases, are printed below the textual notes at the bottom of each page. References to stage directions in the notes follow the admirable system of the Revels editions, whereby stage directions are keyed, decimally, to the line of the text before or after which they occur. Thus, a note on 0.2 has reference to the second line of the stage direction at the beginning of the scene in question. A note on 115.1 has reference to the first line of the stage direction following line 115 of the text of the relevant scene. Speech prefixes, and any stage directions attached to them, are keyed to the first line of accompanying dialogue.

JOHN LOFTIS

Stanford University

Contents

List of Abbreviations

Q1   First Quarto, 1677.

Q2   Second quarto, 1697.

Q3   Third quarto, 1709.

A   First collected edition, 1702.

B   Second ("third") collected edition, 1724.

S   Montague Summers, ed. *The Works of Aphra Behn.* Vol. I. London, 1915.

DG   Dorset Garden Theatre

LIF   Lincoln's Inn Fields Theatre

MLQ   *Modern Language Quarterly*

N & Q   *Notes and Queries*

om.   omitted

PMLA   *Publications of the Modern Language Association*

S.D.   stage direction

S.P.   speech prefix

TR   Theatre Royal, Drury Lane

Introduction

The Rover, Aphra Behn's most famous play, was first published in 1677. Three issues of the first quarto exist, differing only in title page. The title leaf of the first is conjugate with [A4], and may be described as follows:

THE/ ROVER./ OR,/ The Banish't Cavaliers. [black letter]/ [rule]/ As it is ACTED/ AT/ His Royal Highness [black letter]/ THE/ Duke's Theatre./ [rule]/ Licensed *July* 2ᵈ. 1677./ *ROGER L'ESTRANGE.*/ [rule]/ *LONDON,*/ Printed for *John Amery*, at the *Peacock*, against/ St. *Dunstan*'s Church in *Fleet-street*. 1677.

The second issue has a cancel title leaf:

THE/ ROVER:/ OR,/ the Banish't Cavaliers. [black letter]/ [rule]/ A COMEDY:/ ACTED AT/ His Royal Highness [black letter]/ THE/ Duke's Theatre./ [rule]/ Licensed *July* 2d. 1677. *ROGER L'ESTRANGE.*/ [rule]/ *LONDON,*/ Printed for *John Amery*, at the *Peacock*, against/ St. *Dunstan*'s Church in *Fleet-street*. 1677.

The title page of the third issue is also a cancel, and adds the name of the author:

THE/ ROVER:/ OR,/ The Banish't Cavaliers. [black letter]/ [rule]/ A/ COMEDY:/ ACTED AT/ His Royal Highness [black letter]/ THE/ Duke's Theatre./ [rule]/ Written by Mrs. *A. Behn.*/ [rule]/ Licensed *July* 2d. 1677. *ROGER L'ESTRANGE.*/ [rule]/ *LONDON,*/ Printed for *John Amery*, at the *Peacock*, against/ St. *Dunstan*'s Church in *Fleet-street*. 1677.

Two states of the postscript on [M2ʳ] exist, the earlier having nineteen lines, the later twenty, adding the phrase "especially of our sex" after "dominion" in line twenty-three. The Pforzheimer Catalogue remarks that copies were made up without regard to the state of this half sheet, but an examination of nineteen copies shows fourteen first issues, all with the earlier state of the postscript; three second issues, two with the later state and one with the earlier; and two third issues, both with the later. This suggests that the change in the title page of the third issue was either a cause or a consequence of the addition of the phrase to the postscript, and also, with considerably less certainty, that the changes were made after the majority of copies had been run off. Since Q1 was the only edition of the play to appear in Mrs. Behn's lifetime, and since all subsequent editions are derived from it, it is the only authoritative text.

The second quarto (Q2) appeared in 1697, without the postscript. As an inspection of variants will show, it was set from Q1; it corrected few errors and introduced many new ones. The third quarto (Q3) was also set from Q1, and is in general the most accurate text. Published in 1709, it corrects most of the errors in Q1, and introduces remarkably few of its own. Later editions of the single play include an octavo of 1737, a Dublin duodecimo of 1741, and Kemble's alteration of 1790.

The first collected edition of Mrs. Behn's plays (A), printed in 1702 for Tonson and Wellington, appeared before Q3. Each of the two volumes contains four plays, *The Rover* appearing first in Volume I. The text is set from Q2, retaining most of its errors and adding to them. The two volumes were reissued in 1716 in a single volume of what purported to be the "second edition" of the plays, "printed for M. W." Since the text of *The Rover* is in fact identical with that of the 1702 edition, the 1716 issue is of no importance, and was not collated in preparing the present text. "The Third Edition," comprising four volumes, and printed for Mary Poulson, appeared in 1724 (B). The text of *The Rover* was set from A, and is the worst of the early texts. Unfortunately, Pearson's "edition" of Mrs. Behn's works (1871) is as close to a line for line reprint of B as he could produce. Montague Summers also uses the B text, collated casually with Q1 and Q3, in his collected edition of 1915. *The Rover* has thus been available only in a derivative and relatively corrupt text. The present edition is based on Q1, but the substantive variants in Q2, Q3, A, and B have also been recorded.

The Rover belongs to the middle period of Mrs. Behn's dramatic career. She began with *The Forced Marriage* and *The Amorous Prince* (1670 and 1671), two mediocre plays in the popular tradition of Beaumont and Fletcher. Then came *The Dutch Lover* (1673), a play that is hardly better in most respects, though it indicates a shift toward the intrigue comedy and farce which was to occupy her for most of her life. During the season of 1676–1677 at least three, and probably four, of her plays were produced, all at the Dorset Garden Theatre. *Abdelazer* (her only tragedy) and *The Town Fop* belong to the summer and fall of 1676, *The Debauchee* and *The Rover* to the spring of 1677.[1] Although she had borrowed some of the material in both *The Amorous Prince* and *The Dutch Lover*, these four plays initiate a different and more extensive kind of borrowing: they are all adaptations of earlier plays. *The Town Fop* is based on George Wilkins' popular *Miseries of Enforced Marriage*, a wretched piece which Mrs. Behn turns into a fine comedy. *Abdelazer* is based on the anonymous *Lust's Dominion; or, The Lascivious Queen; The Debauchee*, on Brome's *Mad Couple Well Matched*. By the time she came to *The Rover*, then, she was a dramatist with five or six more or less successful plays behind her, and a craftsman experienced in adapting and improving the work of her predecessors.

The Rover, like its sequel *The Second Part of the Rover* (c. 1681), is based on *Thomaso, or, The Wanderer*, a closet drama by Thomas Killigrew. Killigrew's play, written in 1654 and published a decade later in his *Comedies and Tragedies*, is a loosely organized collection of intrigue and farcical plots running to seventy-three scenes in two parts and ten acts. The plots are developed at inordinate length, particularly the farce episodes involving Edwardo (Blunt). Little effort is made to subordinate one to another, or to develop dramatic tension. The speeches are often long, sometimes two or three hundred words, and although often witty, are too unwieldy and slow-moving to be acceptable on the stage. The order brought out of this chaos by Mrs. Behn is obvious to any reader of the two plays.

In the first place, the Blunt episodes are made clearly subordinate to the action involving Willmore and Belvile. Edwardo and Ferdinando become Blunt and Frederick; Lucetta and Phillipo retain their names; Sanco becomes Sancho. The Blunt plot takes up more than eleven scenes in Part One of *Thomaso* alone, and several more in Part Two. Mrs. Behn skilfully condenses and rearranges it, reducing an impossible mass to manageable proportions.

[1.] The authorship of *The Debauchee* has been in doubt, but a strong case for ascribing it to Aphra Behn is presented by Henry A. Hargreaves, "The Life and Plays of Mrs. Behn" (Duke University dissertation, 1961), pp. 260–271.

Willmore, in his gaiety and fondness for amorous pursuits, resembles Thomaso. Killigrew's hero, however, is inconsistent: along with these characteristics he reveals a steady love for Serulina throughout the play, and hence must unconvincingly repent of his unfaithfulness before being united to her. Mrs. Behn removes the inconsistency by embodying in Willmore those traits of Thomaso which will make him the typical gallant of the comedy of wit, and then creating in Belvile a new character whose fidelity contrasts with Willmore's fickleness. Serulina becomes Belvile's Florinda; Hellena, a new character, becomes the eventual partner of the Rover. Angellica Bianca is very much like her counterpart in *Thomaso*, though Mrs. Behn leaves her fate in greater doubt. Killigrew associates her with two other courtesans, who are themselves involved in an elaborate plot in Part Two. Mrs. Behn eliminates this action, and reduces Angellica's part considerably. Antonio, Pedro, and Callis have similar roles in both plays; Valeria, however, is Mrs. Behn's creation, used with Frederick to obtain still a third pair of lovers. The changes lead to economy and dramatic effectiveness, and are nearly always successful.

Mrs. Behn recognizes Killigrew's literary ability, and in matters of style owes him a considerable debt. She follows a number of his scenes rather closely, and frequently incorporates lines from the earlier play in dialogue of her own. This is the more significant in that her usual practice in adaptations was to rewrite. Everywhere, however, she cuts, condenses, reorganizes: though some dialogue closely resembles Killigrew's, much is rewritten completely, or is entirely original. Many of *Thomaso*'s speeches take up half a folio page or more; from the acting point of view, the brisk and racy dialogue of *The Rover* is a refreshing change. It is also worth remarking, since Aphra Behn's reputation for licentiousness is still current, that she follows her usual practice in cutting, lightening, or turning into humor most of the earlier playwright's vulgarity and bawdry.

Her play was first performed at the Duke's Theatre in Dorset Garden in March of 1677. A performance on the twenty-fourth is recorded, and additional ones in 1680, 1685, 1687, and 1690.[2] Theatrical records for this period are scarce; it is likely that there were other performances. Charles II attended on March 24, 1677, and the play was popular not only with him, but with his successors

[2] *The London Stage, 1660–1800*, Part 1: 1660–1700, ed. William Van Lennep (Carbondale, Ill., 1965). It is not known whether the performance on March 24, 1677, was the first; it is the first of which there is record.

as well.³ Smith created the role of Willmore; Cave Underhill that of Ned Blunt. Both became famous in the parts. Betterton and his wife played Belvile and Florinda, Anne Quin played Angellica, and Elizabeth Barry the first Hellena.

The comedy soon became part of the repertoire. Between 1700 and 1725 seventy performances are recorded.⁴ Wilks was the best-known Rover of this era, though the part was also taken by Verbruggen and Powell. Mrs. Oldfield was a famous Hellena, and Mrs. Verbruggen, Mrs. Mountfort, Mrs. Baker, Mrs. Rogers, Mrs. Bradshaw, and Anne Bracegirdle also took the role. Estcourt was acclaimed as Blunt; Mrs. Barry as Angellica. In the second quarter of the century the play was equally popular, some eighty-eight performances being recorded between 1726 and 1760. In the twenties, Wilks usually played Willmore opposite Mrs. Booth; Ryan and Giffard later took the part. Mrs. Vincent most frequently played Hellena, sharing the role between 1737 and 1760 with Peg Woffington. Penkethman, Hall, and the younger Cibber played Blunt in succession to Underhill and Estcourt. After performances at least once a season between 1703 and 1743, and revivals at Covent Garden in 1748 and 1757, the play was seen no more. John Philip Kemble thought it good enough to present in an altered version at Drury Lane in 1790, but *Love in Many Masks* is pale and emasculated beside its original. Times had changed, and the taste of the public called for less frank fare.

The success of *The Rover* is not hard to understand: it had something for everyone. Willmore is the typical gallant, an ardent and penniless cavalier, heedless of danger save to his honor, unabashedly in pursuit of every attractive woman. He loves a challenge like a bottle of sack, and the thousand crowns a month Angellica asks for her favors are no insurmountable obstacle. He also loves his freedom, and expects his women to be as free as he. Angellica is no sooner won than ignored; he must, he tells her, "like cheerful birds, sing in all groves,/ And perch on every bough,/ Billing the next kind she that flies to meet me," and is off to try Hellena. In her, however, he has met his match. She is as witty as she is beautiful; he wins no favors till "old gaffer Hymen and his priest" have secured her future.

³ It was presented by royal command, for example, on April 17, 1724, and on March 13, 1729. Characters in the play frequently refer eulogistically to Charles II.

⁴ *The London Stage*, Parts 2 and 3, provides detailed information about performances between 1700 and 1760.

Though she wins her point, his yoke is to be an easy one: Hellena is a delight, and this is no marriage for "portion and jointure," no marriage arranged to perpetuate a family's name or increase its wealth, but a contract between two free and like-minded people. The dialogues between them provide the best moments in the play, revealing Mrs. Behn's ear for speech rhythms and her talent for witty metaphor. Beatrice and Benedick, and their Jacobean and Caroline successors, come immediately to mind, but Willmore and Hellena are distinctive creations. Like Mirabell and Millamant, their more famous counterparts, they succeed in finding a viable path through the foolish world in which they live; if they lack the elegance of Congreve's lovers, their greater openness and joy in life provide much compensation.

If Willmore and Hellena represent Mrs. Behn's conception of a true love relationship, then Blunt on the one hand and Pedro and Antonio on the other represent unacceptable but conventional alternatives. Blunt is the country squire ubiquitous in the comedy of the period. Like Willmore, he is in search of a woman; but his interests, unlike the Rover's, are simply carnal: women are objects to be bought and sold, love is merely lust. His pursuit of Lucetta parallels in both plot and theme Willmore's of Angellica. Their fates differ, however, because Blunt is only a good-natured fool without the other's intelligence, energy, and wit. He is duped because he deceives himself into thinking that he can get something for nothing, and it takes a trip through the sewer to disillusion him. His loss of clothes and money leaves him both literally and thematically naked, and he comes out of the sewer only to be as foolishly mistaken about Florinda as he was earlier about Lucetta.

Blunt says at one time that he would marry Lucetta were she single, but it is clear that marriage is for him an economic matter: the settlements would cost him money, and Lucetta would not be worth the cost. Here Blunt is aligned with his opposites Pedro and Antonio. These two are young and wealthy men of intelligence and passion. They are stock figures in the comedy of intrigue which Mrs. Behn likes so well; she uses them to motivate the fights in the dark, disguises, mistakes in identity, and so on, which fill the play. Passionate enough about Angellica, they are cool and businesslike about the institution of marriage. Pedro, who alternately urges his sister to marry Antonio and denies her to Belvile, is the image of his father, who wants her to marry the wealthy relict of an ancient house.

Antonio is worse. The thought of marriage to Florinda interferes not at all with his lust for Angellica; yet ironically enough, he thinks to gain both by offering money or its equivalent in property and reputation.

The attack on forced marriage, on matches arranged to gain or perpetuate prestige or economic power, appears frequently in Mrs. Behn's plays. In *The Rover*, however, she derives this theme more carefully than usual from the structure and language of the play. Hellena, for example, uses images which make vivid her feeling that conventional marriage is destructive—as bad a fate as the convent. Willmore is even more suspicious than she: indeed, her problem in the play is to convince him that wedlock need not be this way. The theme is thus centralized in these two characters. Although the country fool of the comedy of wit and the rich and highly placed suitor of the comedy of intrigue come from and represent quite disparate dramatic traditions, they too are made to reinforce the theme. They are the negative exempla to which the pair of true lovers is most strikingly contrasted. The thematic integration of farce, intrigue, and wit is by no means perfect, but Mrs. Behn manages to unify most of the elements making up the play.

Belvile and Florinda also provide a contrast to Willmore and Hellena. In this case, however, the contrast does not involve moral opposition. Mrs. Behn consistently uses in her better comedies a double set of lovers, even in some of the adaptations of originals which, like *Thomaso*, did not have them. Her purpose is dramatic contrast, not of black and white, but of two shades of white. If Willmore and Hellena are superior in wit and vitality, and transform the conventional marriage arrangement to suit themselves, Belvile and Florinda represent those lovers who can function within it because they do not feel any of the threats it poses for the other pair. Belvile cannot understand Willmore's interest in every passing female, or his easy transfer of affection from one to another; even when tempted by Florinda in disguise, he remains constant to her. Florinda, in turn, is shocked by her younger sister, and cannot see how Hellena can love the Rover upon such short acquaintance. Mrs. Behn clearly likes the brilliant pair more than the romantic one, but she uses each to illuminate the other in the course of the action.

The two apparent weaknesses of the play are its excessive reliance on the conventions of intrigue and its failure to resolve adequately the problem of Angellica. Mrs. Behn retained her fondness for the elaborate disguises, duels, mistakes in identity, and farcical gulling made fashionable in England by Tuke's *Adventures of Five Hours*, even after the initial vogue of such conventions had passed. Audiences obviously liked them, and she may well have been attracted by the opportunity they presented for stage spectacle. But though the intrigue elements and the farce are well managed, they are difficult for the modern reader to enjoy. Often they seem merely means of obtaining plot complication and irrelevant spectacular effects.

Angellica, who has a complex literary ancestry extending far beyond *Thomaso*,[5] does not quite fit the comic world of the play. She is a woman of the world, and certainly fair game for the Rover; Willmore does not deceive her with promises of marriage, and her experience is more than sufficient for her to recognize that his interest in her is ephemeral and purely sexual. Yet when she is deserted for Hellena, her sense of rejection and her understanding of her situation are so movingly presented as to take her for the moment out of the comic ethos entirely. She reappears, to be sure, as the traditional scorned woman seeking vengeance, but the shift from a believable and individualized woman to an artificial and conventional type is remarkably unconvincing.

Its weaknesses notwithstanding, *The Rover* is very entertaining. The interest in spectacle is served by well-managed stage business, by the elaborate costuming required in the disguises and masquerades, by the fighting, and by Blunt's trap door. Music and singing provide an additional attraction. And finally, the Rover himself embodies much of the wit, gaiety, and freedom associated with the comedy of the Restoration. Fortunately, the cynicism, amorality, and waste in the lives of many of his historical counterparts need not inhibit our pleasure in the play.

FREDERICK M. LINK

University of Nebraska

[5] Similar characters appear, for example, in Brome's *The Novella*, Marston's *The Dutch Courtesan*, and Dekker's *The Honest Whore*, though Mrs. Behn owes a specific debt only to the first of these.

THE ROVER

PROLOGUE

Wits, like physicians, never can agree,
When of a different society.
And Rabel's drops were never more cried down
By all the learned doctors of the town,
Than a new play whose author is unknown.   5
Nor can those doctors with more malice sue
(And powerful purses) the dissenting few,
Than those, with an insulting pride, do rail
At all who are not of their own cabal.
  If a young poet hit your humor right,   10
You judge him then out of revenge and spite.
So amongst men there are ridiculous elves,
Who monkeys hate for being too like themselves.
So that the reason of the grand debate
Why wit so oft is damned when good plays take,   15
Is that you censure as you love, or hate.
  Thus like a learned conclave poets sit,
Catholic judges both of sense and wit,
And damn or save as they themselves think fit.
Yet those who to others' faults are so severe,   20
Are not so perfect but themselves may err.
Some write correct, indeed, but then the whole
(Bating their own dull stuff i'th' play) is stole:
As bees do suck from flowers their honeydew,
So they rob others striving to please you.   25
  Some write their characters genteel and fine,
But then they do so toil for every line,
That what to you does easy seem, and plain,
Is the hard issue of their laboring brain.
And some th'effects of all their pains, we see,   30
Is but to mimic good extempore.

12. men] *Q1–2, A, B;* them *Q3.*   21. themselves] *Q1, Q3, B;* they
18. and wit] *Q1, Q3, A, B;* of wit   themselves *Q2, A.*
Q2.

---

3. *Rabel's drops*] a well-known patent medicine.
9. *cabal*] secret group.
12. *elves*] malicious persons.
23. *Bating*] excepting.

Others, by long converse about the town,
Have wit enough to write a lewd lampoon,
But their chief skill lies in a bawdy song.
In short, the only wit that's now in fashion,   35
Is but the gleanings of good conversation.
As for the author of this coming play,
I asked him what he thought fit I should say
In thanks for your good company today:
He called me fool, and said it was well known   40
You came not here for our sakes, but your own.
New plays are stuffed with wits, and with deboches,
That crowd and sweat like cits in May-Day coaches.

WRITTEN BY A PERSON OF QUALITY

---

42. *deboches*] debauches.
43. *cits*] ordinary city dwellers; shopkeepers
43. *May-Day coaches*] On May Day it was customary to parade around
Hyde Park.

THE ACTORS' NAMES

[Men]

Don Antonio, the Viceroy's son	*Mr. Jevon*	
Don Pedro, a noble Spaniard, his friend	*Mr. Medbourne*	
Belvile, an English colonel in love with Florinda	*Mr. Betterton*	
Willmore, the Rover	*Mr. Smith*	5
Frederick, an English gentleman, and friend to Belvile and Blunt	*Mr. Crosby*	
Blunt, an English country gentleman	*Mr. Underhill*	
Stephano, servant to Don Pedro	*Mr. Richards*	
Philippo, Lucetta's gallant	*Mr. Percival*	10
Sancho, pimp to Lucetta	*Mr. John Lee*	
Biskey *and* Sebastian, two bravos to Angellica		
Officer *and* Soldiers		
[Diego,] Page to Don Antonio		15

[Women]

Florinda, sister to Don Pedro	*Mrs. Betterton*	
Hellena, a gay young woman designed for a nun, and sister to Florinda	*Mrs. Barry*	
Valeria, a kinswoman to Florinda	*Mrs. Hughes*	
Angellica Bianca, a famous courtesan	*Mrs. Quin*	20
Moretta, her woman	*Mrs. Leigh*	
Callis, governess to Florinda and Hellena	*Mrs. Norris*	
Lucetta, a jilting wench	*Mrs. Gillow*	

Servants, Other Masqueraders, Men and Women

The scene: *Naples, in Carnival time*

7. Blunt] *Q 2, A, B;* Fred. *Q 1, Q 3.*

15. The name is supplied by the S.D. before II.i.

The Rover

or

The Banished Cavaliers

ACT I

[I.i]   *A Chamber.*
Enter Florinda *and* Hellena.

FLORINDA.

   What an impertinent thing is a young girl bred in a nunnery! How full of questions! Prithee no more, Hellena; I
   have told thee more than thou understand'st already.

HELLENA.

   The more's my grief. I would fain know as much as you,
   which makes me so inquisitive; nor is't enough I know   5
   you're a lover, unless you tell me too who 'tis you sigh for.

FLORINDA.

   When you're a lover I'll think you fit for a secret of that
   nature.

HELLENA.

   'Tis true, I never was a lover yet, but I begin to have a
   shrewd guess what 'tis to be so, and fancy it very pretty to   10
   sigh, and sing, and blush, and wish, and dream and wish,
   and long and wish to see the man, and when I do, look pale
   and tremble, just as you did when my brother brought home
   the fine English colonel to see you. What do you call him?
   Don Belvile?   15

FLORINDA.

   Fie, Hellena.

5. I know] *Q1, Q3;* to know *Q2,*
A, B.

HELLENA.

That blush betrays you. I am sure 'tis so. Or is it Don
Antonio the Viceroy's son? Or perhaps the rich old Don
Vincentio, whom my father designs you for a husband? Why
do you blush again?   20

FLORINDA.

With indignation; and how near soever my father thinks I
am to marrying that hated object, I shall let him see I
understand better what's due to my beauty, birth, and
fortune, and more to my soul, than to obey those unjust
commands.   25

HELLENA.

Now hang me, if I don't love thee for that dear disobedience.
I love mischief strangely, as most of our sex do who are come
to love nothing else. But tell me, dear Florinda, don't you
love that fine *Anglese*? For I vow, next to loving him myself,
'twill please me most that you do so, for he is so gay and so   30
handsome.

FLORINDA.

Hellena, a maid designed for a nun ought not to be so curious
in a discourse of love.

HELLENA.

And dost thou think that ever I'll be a nun? Or at least till I'm
so old I'm fit for nothing else? Faith no, sister; and that   35
which makes me long to know whether you love Belvile, is
because I hope he has some mad companion or other that
will spoil my devotion. Nay, I'm resolved to provide myself
this Carnival, if there be e'er a handsome proper fellow of
my humor above ground, though I ask first.   40

FLORINDA.

Prithee be not so wild.

HELLENA.

Now you have provided yourself of a man you take no care
of poor me. Prithee tell me, what dost thou see about me
that is unfit for love? Have I not a world of youth? A
humor gay? A beauty passable? A vigor desirable? Well   45

19. designs you for a] *Q1, Q3;*   39. proper] *Q1–3; om. A, B.*
designs for your *Q2, A, B.*   42. of a] *Q1, Q3;* with a *Q2, A, B.*

29. *Anglese*] Englishman.
32. *curious*] inquisitive.

shaped? Clean limbed? Sweet breathed? And sense enough
to know how all these ought to be employed to the best
advantage? Yes, I do and will; therefore lay aside your
hopes of my fortune by my being a devote, and tell me how
you came acquainted with this Belvile. For I perceive you   50
knew him before he came to Naples.

FLORINDA.

Yes, I knew him at the siege of Pamplona; he was then a
colonel of French horse, who when the town was ransacked,
nobly treated my brother and myself, preserving us from
all insolences. And I must own, besides great obligations, I   55
have I know not what that pleads kindly for him about my
heart, and will suffer no other to enter. But see, my brother.

Enter Don Pedro, Stephano *with a masking habit, and* Callis.

PEDRO.

Good morrow, sister. Pray when saw you your lover Don
Vincentio?

FLORINDA.

I know not, sir. Callis, when was he here? For I consider it   60
so little I know not when it was.

PEDRO.

I have a command from my father here to tell you you ought
not to despise him, a man of so vast a fortune, and such a
passion for you. —Stephano, my things.

Puts on his masking habit.

FLORINDA.

A passion for me? 'Tis more than e'er I saw, or he had a   65
desire should be known. I hate Vincentio, sir, and I would
not have a man so dear to me as my brother follow the ill
customs of our country and make a slave of his sister. And,
sir, my father's will I'm sure you may divert.

57. But see] *Q1, Q3, A, B;* But to   65. he] *Q1, Q3; om. Q2, A, B.*
see *Q2.*   66. sir] *Q1, Q3; om. Q2, A, B.*
64. my things] *Q1, Q3;* m'thinks
Q2; methinks *A, B.*

49. *devote*] nun.
52. *Pamplona*] fortified capital of Navarre, often under siege.
53. *horse*] cavalry.
57.1. *masking habit*] masquerade costume.

PEDRO.

I know not how dear I am to you, but I wish only to be 70
ranked in your esteem equal with the English colonel Belvile.
Why do you frown and blush? Is there any guilt belongs to
the name of that cavalier?

FLORINDA.

I'll not deny I value Belvile. When I was exposed to such
dangers as the licenced lust of common soldiers threatened 75
when rage and conquest flew through the city, then Belvile,
this criminal for my sake, threw himself into all dangers to
save my honor. And will you not allow him my esteem?

PEDRO.

Yes, pay him what you will in honor, but you must consider
Don Vincentio's fortune, and the jointure he'll make you. 80

FLORINDA.

Let him consider my youth, beauty, and fortune, which
ought not to be thrown away on his age and jointure.

PEDRO.

'Tis true, he's not so young and fine a gentleman as that
Belvile. But what jewels will that cavalier present you with?
Those of his eyes and heart? 85

HELLENA.

And are not those better than any Don Vincentio has
brought from the Indies?

PEDRO.

Why, how now! Has your nunnery breeding taught you to
understand the value of hearts and eyes?

HELLENA.

Better than to believe Vincentio's deserve value from any 90
woman. He may perhaps increase her bags, but not her
family.

PEDRO.

This is fine! Go! Up to your devotion! You are not designed
for the conversation of lovers.

77. threw] *Q3, A, B;* through *Q1-2.*   tio deserves *A, B.*
90. Vincentio's deserve] *Q1, Q3;*   93. devotion] *Q1-2, A, B;* devo-
Vincentio's deserves *Q2;* Vincen-   tions *Q3.*

---

80. *jointure*] estate settled on a wife in lieu of dower.
91. *bags*] wealth, possibly with a pun on the use of the phrase to mean
"make her pregnant."

HELLENA (*aside*).

Nor saints yet a while, I hope. —Is't not enough you make 95
a nun of me, but you must cast my sister away too, exposing
her to a worse confinement than a religious life?

PEDRO.

The girl's mad! It is a confinement to be carried into the
country to an ancient villa belonging to the family of the
Vincentios these five hundred years, and have no other 100
prospect than that pleasing one of seeing all her own that
meets her eyes: a fine air, large fields, and gardens where
she may walk and gather flowers?

HELLENA.

When, by moonlight? For I am sure she dares not encounter
with the heat of the sun; that were a task only for Don 105
Vincentio and his Indian breeding, who loves it in the dog
days. And if these be her daily divertissements, what are
those of the night? To lie in a wide moth-eaten bedchamber
with furniture in fashion in the reign of King Sancho the
First; the bed, that which his forefathers lived and died in. 110

PEDRO.

Very well.

HELLENA.

This apartment, new furbrushed and fitted out for the
young wife, he out of freedom makes his dressing room; and
being a frugal and a jealous coxcomb, instead of a valet to
uncase his feeble carcass, he desires you to do that office. 115
Signs of favor, I'll assure you, and such as you must not hope
for unless your woman be out of the way.

PEDRO.

Have you done yet?

HELLENA.

That honor being past, the giant stretches itself, yawns and
sighs a belch or two loud as a musket, throws himself into 120

98. It is] *Q 1–2;* Is it *Q 3, A, B.*   120. loud] *Q 1–3;* as loud *A, B.*
119. itself] *Q 1–2, A, B;* himself *Q 3.*

106–107. *dog days*] sultry part of summer.
109. *Sancho*] probably of Navarre (tenth century).
112. *furbrushed*] renovated.
115. *uncase*] undress.

bed, and expects you in his foul sheets; and ere you can get
yourself undressed, calls you with a snore or two. And are not
these fine blessings to a young lady?

PEDRO.

Have you done yet?

HELLENA.

And this man you must kiss, nay you must kiss none but him 125
too, and nuzzle through his beard to find his lips. And this
you must submit to for threescore years, and all for a
jointure.

PEDRO.

For all your character of Don Vincentio, she is as like to
marry him as she was before.   130

HELLENA.

Marry Don Vincentio! Hang me, such a wedlock would be
worse than adultery with another man. I had rather see her
in the *Hostel de Dieu*, to waste her youth there in vows, and
be a handmaid to lazars and cripples, than to lose it in such
a marriage.   135

PEDRO.

You have considered, sister, that Belvile has no fortune to
bring you to; banished his country, despised at home, and
pitied abroad.

HELLENA.

What then? The Viceroy's son is better than that old Sir
Fifty. Don Vincentio! Don Indian! He thinks he's trading 140
to Gambo still, and would barter himself—that bell and
bauble—for your youth and fortune.

PEDRO.

Callis, take her hence and lock her up all this Carnival,
and at Lent she shall begin her everlasting penance in a
monastery.   145

HELLENA.

I care not; I had rather be a nun than be obliged to marry
as you would have me if I were designed for't.

---

133. *Hostel de Dieu*] hospital operated by a religious order.
134. *lazars*] paupers inflicted with a pestilent disease.
141. *Gambo*] British colony in West Africa.
141–142. *bell and bauble*] trifle.

PEDRO.

Do not fear the blessing of that choice. You shall be a nun.

HELLENA (*aside*).

Shall I so? You may chance to be mistaken in my way of
devotion. A nun! Yes, I am like to make a fine nun! I have 150
an excellent humor for a grate! No, I'll have a saint of my
own to pray to shortly, if I like any that dares venture on me.

PEDRO.

Callis, make it your business to watch this wildcat. —As for
you, Florinda, I've only tried you all this while and urged my
father's will; but mine is that you would love Antonio: he 155
is brave and young, and all that can complete the happiness
of a gallant maid. This absence of my father will give us
opportunity to free you from Vincentio by marrying here,
which you must do tomorrow.

FLORINDA.

Tomorrow!   160

PEDRO.

Tomorrow, or 'twill be too late. 'Tis not my friendship to
Antonio which makes me urge this, but love to thee and
hatred to Vincentio; therefore resolve upon tomorrow.

FLORINDA.

Sir, I shall strive to do as shall become your sister.

PEDRO.

I'll both believe and trust you. Adieu.   165

                                    Exeunt Pedro *and* Stephano.

HELLENA.

As becomes his sister! That is to be as resolved your way as
he is his.   Hellena *goes to* Callis.

FLORINDA.

I ne'er till now perceived my ruin near.
I've no defence against Antonio's love,
For he has all the advantages of nature,   170
The moving arguments of youth and fortune.

163. upon] *Q1-3;* upon't *A, B.*   *Q2, A, B.*
166. becomes] *Q1, Q3;* become   168. ne'er] *Q1-3, B;* near *A.*

151. *grate*] lattice barring convent window.

HELLENA.

But hark you, Callis, you will not be so cruel to lock me up
indeed, will you?

CALLIS.

I must obey the commands I have. Besides, do you consider what a life you are going to lead?   175

HELLENA.

Yes, Callis, that of a nun; and till then I'll be indebted a
world of prayers to you if you'll let me now see what I never
did, the divertissements of a Carnival.

CALLIS.

What, go in masquerade? 'Twill be a fine farewell to the
world, I take it. Pray what would you do there?   180

HELLENA.

That which all the world does, as I am told: be as mad as
the rest and take all innocent freedoms. Sister, you'll go too,
will you not? Come, prithee be not sad. We'll outwit twenty
brothers if you'll be ruled by me. Come, put off this dull
humor with your clothes, and assume one as gay and as   185
fantastic as the dress my cousin Valeria and I have provided,
and let's ramble.

FLORINDA.

Callis, will you give us leave to go?

CALLIS (aside).

I have a youthful itch of going myself. —Madam, if I
thought your brother might not know it, and I might wait   190
on you; for by my troth I'll not trust young girls alone.

FLORINDA.

Thou seest my brother's gone already, and thou shalt attend
and watch us.

Enter Stephano.

STEPHANO.

Madam, the habits are come, and your cousin Valeria is
dressed and stays for you.   195

174. have] *Q1, Q3;* hate *Q2, A, B.*   194. Madam,] *Q3, B;* Mad? *Q1;*
                                              Mad! *Q2, A.*

FLORINDA [*aside*].

'Tis well. I'll write a note, and if I chance to see Belvile and want an opportunity to speak to him, that shall let him know what I've resolved in favor of him.

HELLENA.

Come, let's in and dress us. *Exeunt.*

[I.ii] *A long street.*
Enter Belvile, *melancholy;* Blunt *and* Frederick.

FREDERICK.

Why, what the devil ails the colonel, in a time when all the world is gay to look like mere Lent thus? Hadst thou been long enough in Naples to have been in love, I should have sworn some such judgment had befallen thee.

BELVILE.

No, I have made no new amours since I came to Naples. 5

FREDERICK.

You have left none behind you in Paris?

BELVILE.

Neither.

FREDERICK.

I cannot divine the cause then, unless the old cause, the want of money.

BLUNT.

And another old cause, the want of a wench. Would not 10 that revive you?

BELVILE.

You are mistaken, Ned.

BLUNT.

Nay, 'adsheartlikins, then thou'rt past cure.

FREDERICK.

I have found it out: thou hast renewed thy acquaintance with the lady that cost thee so many sighs at the siege of 15 Pamplona—pox on't, what d'ye call her—her brother's a noble Spaniard, nephew to the dead general. Florinda. Ay, Florinda. And will nothing serve thy turn but that damned virtuous woman, whom on my conscience thou lov'st in spite too, because thou seest little or no possibility of gaining her. 20

BELVILE.

Thou art mistaken; I have int'rest enough in that lovely
virgin's heart to make me proud and vain, were it not
abated by the severity of a brother, who, perceiving my
happiness—

FREDERICK.

Has civilly forbid thee the house?   25

BELVILE.

'Tis so, to make way for a powerful rival, the Viceroy's son,
who has the advantage of me in being a man of fortune, a
Spaniard, and her brother's friend; which gives him liberty
to make his court, whilst I have recourse only to letters and
distant looks from her window, which are as soft and kind   30
As those which heaven sends down on penitents.

BLUNT.

Heyday! 'Adsheartlikins, simile! By this light the man is
quite spoiled. Fred, what the devil are we made of that we
cannot be thus concerned for a wench? 'Adsheartlikins, our
Cupids are like the cooks of the camp: they can roast or boil   35
a woman, but they have none of the fine tricks to set 'em off;
no hogoes to make the sauce pleasant and the stomach
sharp.

FREDERICK.

I dare swear I have had a hundred as young, kind, and
handsome as this Florinda; and dogs eat me if they were not   40
as troublesome to me i'th' morning as they were welcome
o'er night.

BLUNT.

And yet I warrant he would not touch another woman if he
might have her for nothing.

BELVILE.

That's thy joy, a cheap whore.   45

BLUNT.

Why, 'adsheartlikins, I love a frank soul. When did you
ever hear of an honest woman that took a man's money? I

31.] *Q1; prose Q2, A, B; prose ital.*   36. the fine] *Q1–2, A, B; these fine*
Q3.   *Q3.*

---

37. *hogoes*] relishes, savories.

warrant 'em good ones. But gentlemen, you may be free;
you have been kept so poor with parliaments and protectors
that the little stock you have is not worth preserving. But I   50
thank my stars I had more grace than to forfeit my estate by
cavaliering.

BELVILE.

Methinks only following the court should be sufficient to
entitle 'em to that.

BLUNT.

'Adsheartlikins, they know I follow it to do it no good,   55
unless they pick a hole in my coat for lending you money
now and then, which is a greater crime to my conscience,
gentlemen, than to the commonwealth.

Enter Willmore.

WILLMORE.

Ha! Dear Belvile! Noble colonel!

BELVILE.

Willmore! Welcome ashore, my dear rover! What happy   60
wind blew us this good fortune?

WILLMORE.

Let me salute my dear Fred, and then command me. —How
is't, honest lad?

FREDERICK.

Faith, sir, the old compliment, infinitely the better to see my
dear mad Willmore again. Prithee, why camest thou ashore?   65
And where's the Prince?

WILLMORE.

He's well, and reigns still lord of the wat'ry element. I must
aboard again within a day or two, and my business ashore
was only to enjoy myself a little this Carnival.

BELVILE.

Pray know our new friend, sir; he's but bashful, a raw   70
traveler, but honest, stout, and one of us.

Embraces Blunt.

WILLMORE.

That you esteem him gives him an int'rest here.

51–52. *forfeit . . . cavaliering*] Cromwell confiscated many Royalist estates.
66. *Prince*] Charles II.

BLUNT.

Your servant, sir.

WILLMORE.

But well, faith, I'm glad to meet you again in a warm
climate, where the kind sun has its godlike power still over   75
the wine and women. Love and mirth are my business in
Naples, and if I mistake not the place, here's an excellent
market for chapmen of my humor.

BELVILE.

See, here be those kind merchants of love you look for.

*Enter several men in masking habits, some playing on music, others dancing
after; women dressed like courtesans, with papers pinned on their breasts, and
baskets of flowers in their hands.*

BLUNT.

'Adsheartlikins, what have we here?   80

FREDERICK.

Now the game begins.

WILLMORE.

Fine pretty creatures! May a stranger have leave to look
and love? What's here? "Roses for every month"?

Reads the papers.

BLUNT.

Roses for every month? What means that?

BELVILE.

They are, or would have you think they're courtesans, who   85
here in Naples are to be hired by the month.

WILLMORE.

Kind and obliging to inform us, pray where do these roses
grow? I would fain plant some of 'em in a bed of mine.

WOMAN.

Beware such roses, sir.

WILLMORE.

A pox of fear: I'll be baked with thee between a pair of   90
sheets, and that's thy proper still; so I might but strew such
roses over me and under me. Fair one, would you would

83.1 *papers*] *Q1–3; paper A, B.*   91. strew] *Q1–3; strow A, B.*

---

78. *chapmen*] merchants.
91. *still*] fill? (Unclear.)

give me leave to gather at your bush this idle month; I
would go near to make somebody smell of it all the year
after.   95

BELVILE.

And thou hast need of such a remedy, for thou stink'st of
tar and ropes' ends like a dock or pesthouse.

The Woman puts herself into the hands of a man and exeunt.

WILLMORE.

Nay, nay, you shall not leave me so.

BELVILE.

By all means use no violence here.

WILLMORE.

Death! Just as I was going to be damnably in love, to have 100
her led off! I could pluck that rose out of his hand, and even
kiss the bed the bush grew in.

FREDERICK.

No friend to love like a long voyage at sea.

BLUNT.

Except a nunnery, Fred.

WILLMORE.

Death! But will they not be kind? Quickly be kind? Thou 105
know'st I'm no tame sigher, but a rampant lion of the
forest.

*Advances from the farther end of the scenes two men dressed all over with
horns of several sorts, making grimaces at one another, with papers pinned on
their backs.*

BELVILE.

Oh the fantastical rogues, how they're dressed! 'Tis a
satire against the whole sex.

WILLMORE.

Is this a fruit that grows in this warm country?   110

BELVILE.

Yes, 'tis pretty to see these Italians start, swell, and stab at
the word cuckold, and yet stumble at horns on every
threshold.

102. bush] *Q1, Q3;* bush it *Q2, A,*
B.

---

97. *pesthouse*] shelter for those inflicted with pestilence.
107.2. *horns*] traditional sign of the cuckold.

WILLMORE.

> See what's on their back. (*Reads*). "Flowers of every
> night." Ah, rógue! And more sweet than roses of every 115
> month! This is a gardener of Adam's own breeding.
>
> > *They dance.*

BELVILE.

> What think you of these grave people? Is a wake in Essex
> half so mad or extravagant?

WILLMORE.

> I like their sober grave way; 'tis a kind of legal authorized
> fornication, where the men are not chid for't, nor the 120
> women despised, as amongst our dull English. Even the
> monsieurs want that part of good manners.

BELVILE.

> But here in Italy, a monsieur is the humblest best-bred
> gentleman: duels are so baffled by bravos that an age
> shows not one but between a Frenchman and a hangman, 125
> who is as much too hard for him on the Piazza as they are
> for a Dutchman on the New Bridge. But see, another crew.

Enter Florinda, Hellena, *and* Valeria, *dressed like gipsies;* Callis *and*
Stephano, Lucetta, Philippo *and* Sancho *in masquerade.*

HELLENA.

> Sister, there's your Englishman, and with him a handsome
> proper fellow. I'll to him, and instead of telling him his for-
> tune, try my own.   130

WILLMORE.

> Gipsies, on my life. Sure these will prattle if a man cross
> their hands. (*Goes to* Hellena.) —Dear, pretty, and, I
> hope, young devil, will you tell an amorous stranger what
> luck he's like to have?

HELLENA.

> Have a care how you venture with me, sir, lest I pick your 135

---

122. *monsieurs*] the French.
124. *bravos*] hired ruffians or assassins.
126. *Piazza*] large open square.
127. *Dutchman . . . Bridge*] a reference to French successes in Flanders
during the Commonwealth period?
131–132. *cross their hands*] give them money.

pocket, which will more vex your English humor than an
Italian fortune will please you.

WILLMORE.

How the devil cam'st thou to know my country and humor?

HELLENA.

The first I guess by a certain forward impudence, which does
not displease me at this time; and the loss of your money 140
will vex you because I hope you have but very little to lose.

WILLMORE.

Egad, child, thou'rt i'th' right; it is so little I dare not offer
it thee for a kindness. But cannot you divine what other
things of more value I have about me that I would more
willingly part with?   145

HELLENA.

Indeed no, that's the business of a witch, and I am but a
gipsy yet. Yet without looking in your hand, I have a
parlous guess 'tis some foolish heart you mean, an inconstant
English heart, as little worth stealing as your purse.

WILLMORE.

Nay, then thou dost deal with the devil, that's certain. 150
Thou hast guessed as right as if thou hadst been one of that
number it has languished for. I find you'll be better acquainted with it, nor can you take it in a better time; for I am
come from sea, child, and Venus not being propitious to me
in her own element, I have a world of love in store. Would 155
you would be good-natured and take some on't off my
hands.

HELLENA.

Why, I could be inclined that way, but for a foolish vow I
am going to make to die a maid.

WILLMORE.

Then thou art damned without redemption, and as I am a 160
good Christian, I ought in charity to divert so wicked a
design. Therefore prithee, dear creature, let me know
quickly when and where I shall begin to set a helping hand
to so good a work.

HELLENA.

If you should prevail with my tender heart, as I begin to 165
fear you will, for you have horrible loving eyes, there will be
difficulty in't that you'll hardly undergo for my sake.

WILLMORE.

Faith, child, I have been bred in dangers, and wear a
sword that has been employed in a worse cause than for a
handsome kind woman. Name the danger; let it be any- 170
thing but a long siege, and I'll undertake it.

HELLENA.

Can you storm?

WILLMORE.

Oh, most furiously.

HELLENA.

What think you of a nunnery wall? For he that wins me
must gain that first.   175

WILLMORE.

A nun! Oh, now I love thee for't! There's no sinner like a
young saint. Nay, now there's no denying me; the old law
had no curse to a woman like dying a maid: witness
Jeptha's daughter.

HELLENA.

A very good text this, if well handled; and I perceive, Father 180
Captain, you would impose no severe penance on her who
were inclined to console herself before she took orders.

WILLMORE.

If she be young and handsome.

HELLENA.

Ay, there's it. But if she be not—

WILLMORE.

By this hand, child, I have an implicit faith, and dare ven- 185
ture on thee with all faults. Besides, 'tis more meritorious to
leave the world when thou hast tasted and proved the
pleasure on't. Then 'twill be a virtue in thee, which now will
be pure ignorance.

---

171. a long] *Q1–3, B;* along *A.*   182. were] *Q1, Q3;* was *Q2, A, B.*
178. dying a] *Q1, Q3, B;* a dying   188. on't. Then] *Q1, Q3;* on't,
Q2, A.   than *Q2, A, B.*

---

179. *Jeptha's daughter*] See Judges 11:37–40. Before sacrificing her in
fulfillment of a vow, Jeptha allowed her four days to lament her
virginity.
182. *took orders*] became a nun.

HELLENA.

I perceive, good Father Captain, you design only to make 190
me fit for heaven. But if, on the contrary, you should quite
divert me from it, and bring me back to the world again, I
should have a new man to seek, I find. And what a grief that
will be; for when I begin, I fancy I shall love like anything;
I never tried yet.   195

WILLMORE.

Egad, and that's kind! Prithee, dear creature, give me
credit for a heart, for faith, I'm a very honest fellow. Oh, I
long to come first to the banquet of love! And such a swinging appetite I bring. Oh, I'm impatient. Thy lodging, sweetheart, thy lodging, or I'm a dead man!   200

HELLENA.

Why must we be either guilty of fornication or murder if
we converse with you men? And is there no difference
between leave to love me, and leave to lie with me?

WILLMORE.

Faith, child, they were made to go together.

LUCETTA (*pointing to* Blunt).

Are you sure this is the man?   205

SANCHO.

When did I mistake your game?

LUCETTA.

This is a stranger, I know by his gazing; if he be brisk he'll
venture to follow me, and then, if I understand my trade,
he's mine. He's English, too, and they say that's a sort of
good-natured loving people, and have generally so kind an 210
opinion of themselves that a woman with any wit may
flatter 'em into any sort of fool she pleases.

She often passes by Blunt *and gazes on him; he struts and cocks, and walks
and gazes on her.*

BLUNT.

'Tis so, she is taken; I have beauties which my false glass at
home did not discover.

212.1–2.] *Q 1–3; S.D. follows l. 214*
in A, B.

198–199. *swinging*] capital, excellent.

FLORINDA (*aside*).

    This woman watches me so, I shall get no opportunity to 215
discover myself to him, and so miss the intent of my coming.
—[*To* Belvile.]   But as I was saying, sir, by this line you
should be a lover.

                                  Looking in his hand.

BELVILE.

    I thought how right you guessed: all men are in love, or
pretend to be so. Come, let me go; I'm weary of this fooling. 220

                                        Walks away.

FLORINDA.

    I will not, sir, till you have confessed whether the passion
that you have vowed Florinda be true or false.

               She holds him; he strives to get from her.

BELVILE.

    Florinda!   *Turns quick towards her.*

FLORINDA.

    Softly.

BELVILE.

    Thou hast nam'd one will fix me here forever.   225

FLORINDA.

    She'll be disappointed then, who expects you this night at
the garden gate. And if you fail not, as— (*Looks on* Callis,
who observes 'em.)   Let me see the other hand—you will go
near to do, she vows to die or make you happy.

BELVILE.

    What canst thou mean?   230

FLORINDA.

    That which I say. Farewell.   *Offers to go.*

BEVILE.

    Oh charming sybil, stay; complete that joy which as it is
will turn into distraction! Where must I be? At the garden
gate? I know it. At night, you say? I'll sooner forfeit
heaven than disobey.   235

     Enter Don Pedro *and other maskers, and pass over the stage.*

CALLIS.

    Madam, your brother's here.

---

227. you] *Q1–3;* you'll *A, B.*   227.] *S.D. follows speech, Q1–3, A, B.*

FLORINDA.

Take this to instruct you farther.   *Gives him a letter, and goes off.*

FREDERICK.

Have a care, sir, what you promise; this may be a trap laid
by her brother to ruin you.

BELVILE.

Do not disturb my happiness with doubts.   240

Opens the letter.

WILLMORE.

My dear pretty creature, a thousand blessings on thee!
Still in this habit, you say? And after dinner at this place?

HELLENA.

Yes, if you will swear to keep your heart and not bestow it
between this and that.

WILLMORE.

By all the little gods of love, I swear; I'll leave it with you, 245
and if you run away with it, those deities of justice will
revenge me.   *Exeunt all the women [except* Lucetta].

FREDERICK.

Do you know the hand?

BEVILE.

'Tis Florinda's.

All blessings fall upon the virtuous maid.   250

FREDERICK.

Nay, no idolatry; a sober sacrifice I'll allow you.

BELVILE.

Oh friends, the welcom'st news! The softest letter! Nay, you
shall all see it! And could you now be serious, I might be
made the happiest man the sun shines on!

WILLMORE.

The reason of this mighty joy?   255

BELVILE.

See how kindly she invites me to deliver her from the
threatened violence of her brother. Will you not assist me?

WILLMORE.

I know not what thou mean'st, but I'll make one at any
mischief where a woman's concerned. But she'll be grateful
to us for the favor, will she not?   260

253. all] *Q 1–3; om. A, B.*

BELVILE.

How mean you?

WILLMORE.

How should I mean? Thou know'st there's but one way for
a woman to oblige me.

BELVILE.

Do not profane; the maid is nicely virtuous.

WILLMORE.

Who, pox, then she's fit for nothing but a husband. Let her 265
e'en go, colonel.

FREDERICK.

Peace, she's the colonel's mistress, sir.

WILLMORE.

Let her be the devil; if she be thy mistress, I'll serve her.
Name the way.

BELVILE.

Read here this postscript.   *Gives him a letter.* 270

WILLMORE (*reads*).

"At ten at night, at the garden gate, of which, if I cannot
get the key, I will contrive a way over the wall. Come
attended with a friend or two." —Kind heart, if we three
cannot weave a string to let her down a garden wall, 'twere
pity but the hangman wove one for us all.   275

FREDERICK.

Let her alone for that; your woman's wit, your fair kind
woman, will out-trick a broker or a Jew, and contrive like
a Jesuit in chains. But see, Ned Blunt is stolen out after the
lure of a damsel.   *Exeunt* Blunt *and* Lucetta.

BELVILE.

So, he'll scarce find his way home again unless we get him 280
cried by the bellman in the market place. And 'twould
sound prettily: "A lost English boy of thirty."

FREDERICK.

I hope 'tis some common crafty sinner, one that will fit him.
It may be she'll sell him for Peru: the rogue's sturdy, and

277. broker] *Q1, Q3;* brother *Q2,*
A, B.

---

281. *bellman*] town crier.

would work well in a mine. At least I hope she'll dress him 285
for our mirth, cheat him of all, then have him well-favoredly
banged, and turned out at midnight.

WILLMORE.

Prithee what humor is he of, that you wish him so well?

BELVILE.

Why, of an English elder brother's humor: educated in a
nursery, with a maid to tend him till fifteen, and lies with his 290
grandmother till he's of age; one that knows no pleasure
beyond riding to the next fair, or going up to London with
his right worshipful father in parliament time, wearing gay
clothes, or making honorable love to his lady mother's
laundry maid; gets drunk at a hunting match, and ten to 295
one then gives some proofs of his prowess. A pox upon him,
he's our banker, and has all our cash about him; and if he
fail, we are all broke.

FREDERICK.

Oh, let him alone for that matter; he's of a damned stingy
quality that will secure our stock. I know not in what danger 300
it were indeed if the jilt should pretend she's in love with him,
for 'tis a kind believing coxcomb; otherwise, if he part with
more than a piece of eight, geld him—for which offer he may
chance to be beaten if she be a whore of the first rank.

BELVILE.

Nay, the rogue will not be easily beaten; he's stout enough. 305
Perhaps if they talk beyond his capacity he may chance to
exercise his courage upon some of them, else I'm sure they'll
find it as difficult to beat as to please him.

WILLMORE.

'Tis a lucky devil to light upon so kind a wench!

FREDERICK.

Thou hadst a great deal of talk with thy little gipsy; couldst 310
thou do no good upon her? For mine was hardhearted.

WILLMORE.

Hang her, she was some damned honest person of quality,
I'm sure, she was so very free and witty. If her face be but
answerable to her wit and humor, I would be bound to

---

303. *piece of eight*] Spanish dollar.

constancy this month to gain her. In the meantime, have 315
you made no kind acquaintance since you came to town?
You do not use to be honest so long, gentlemen.

FREDERICK.

Faith, love has kept us honest: we have been all fir'd with
a beauty newly come to town, the famous Paduana Angellica Bianca.   320

WILLMORE.

What, the mistress of the dead Spanish general?

BELVILE.

Yes, she's now the only ador'd beauty of all the youth in
Naples, who put on all their charms to appear lovely in her
sight: their coaches, liveries, and themselves all gay as on a
monarch's birthday to attract the eyes of this fair charmer, 325
while she has the pleasure to behold all languish for her that
see her.

FREDERICK.

'Tis pretty to see with how much love the men regard her,
and how much envy the women.

WILLMORE.

What gallant has she?   330

BELVILE.

None; she's exposed to sale, and four days in the week she's
yours, for so much a month.

WILLMORE.

The very thought of it quenches all manner of fire in me.
Yet prithee, let's see her.

BELVILE.

Let's first to dinner, and after that we'll pass the day as you 335
please. But at night ye must all be at my devotion.

WILLMORE.

I will not fail you.   [*Exeunt.*]

The End of the First Act.

337. *S.D. Exeunt*] *Q3, A, B; om.*   336.1.] *In Q1–2; om. Q3, A, B.*
Q1–2.

---

317. *honest*] chaste.
319. *Paduana*] native of Padua.
324–325. *gay . . . birthday*] It was customary to dress finely for the king's
birthday.

ACT II

[II.i]   *The long street.*

Enter Belvile *and* Frederick *in masking habits, and* Willmore *in his own clothes, with a vizard in his hand.*

WILLMORE.
But why thus disguised and muzzled?

BELVILE.
Because whatever extravagances we commit in these faces, our own may not be obliged to answer 'em.

WILLMORE.
I should have changed my eternal buff, too; but no matter, my little gipsy would not have found me out then. For if she   5
should change hers, it is impossible I should know her unless I should hear her prattle. A pox on't, I cannot get her out of my head. Pray heaven, if ever I do see her again, she prove damnably ugly, that I may fortify myself against her tongue.   10

BELVILE.
Have a care of love, for o' my conscience she was not of a quality to give thee any hopes.

WILLMORE.
Pox on 'em, why do they draw a man in then? She has played with my heart so, that 'twill never lie still till I have met with some kind wench that will play the game out with   15
me. Oh, for my arms full of soft, white, kind woman—such as I fancy Angellica.

BELVILE.
This is her house, if you were but in stock to get admittance. They have not dined yet; I perceive the picture is not out.

                    Enter Blunt.

WILLMORE.
I long to see the shadow of the fair substance; a man may   20
gaze on that for nothing.

7. hear] *Q1, Q3, B;* here *Q2, A.*   9. damnably] *Q1;* damnable *Q2-3,*
                                                                    A, B.

0.3. *vizard*] face mask.
4. *buff*] leather military coat.
19. *picture*] See II.i.98.1.

BLUNT.

Colonel, thy hand. And thine, Fred. I have been an ass, a
deluded fool, a very coxcomb from my birth till this hour,
and heartily repent my little faith.

BELVILE.

What the devil's the matter with thee, Ned?   25

BLUNT.

Oh, such a mistress, Fred! Such a girl!

WILLMORE.

Ha! Where?

FREDERICK.

Ay, where?

BLUNT.

So fond, so amorous, so toying, and so fine! And all for
sheer love, ye rogue! Oh, how she looked and kissed! And   30
soothed my heart from my bosom! I cannot think I was
awake, and yet methinks I see and feel her charms still.
Fred, try if she have not left the taste of her balmy kisses
upon my lips.   *Kisses him.*

BELVILE.

Ha! Ha! Ha!   35

WILLMORE.

Death, man, where is she?

BLUNT.

What a dog was I to stay in dull England so long! How
have I laughed at the colonel when he sighed for love! But
now the little archer has revenged him! And by this one
dart I can guess at all his joys, which then I took for fancies, 40
mere dreams and fables. Well, I'm resolved to sell all in
Essex and plant here forever.

BELVILE.

What a blessing 'tis, thou hast a mistress thou dar'st boast
of; for I know thy humor is rather to have a proclaimed
clap than a secret amour.   45

---

26. S.P. BLUNT] *Q3, B; om.*
Q1–2, A.
28.] *S.P. and speech run on with l. 27,*
Q1–3, A, B.
29. S.P. BLUNT] *Q3, A, B; om.*
Q1–2.
29. so fine] *Q1, Q3; fine Q2, A, B.*

36.] *Q3; S.P. and speech run on with*
l. 35, Q1–2, A, B.
37. S.P. BLUNT] *Q3, A, B; om. Q1–*
2.
39. this one] *Q1, Q3; his one Q2,*
A; his own B.
44. a] *Q1–2, A, B; om. Q3.*

WILLMORE.

Dost know her name?

BLUNT.

Her name? No, 'adsheartlikins. What care I for names? She's fair, young, brisk and kind, even to ravishment! And what a pox care I for knowing her by any other title?

WILLMORE.

Didst give her anything?   50

BLUNT.

Give her? Ha! Ha! Ha! Why, she's a person of quality. That's a good one! Give her? 'Adsheartlikins, dost think such creatures are to be bought? Or are we provided for such a purchase? Give her, quoth ye? Why, she presented me with this bracelet for the toy of a diamond I used to   55 wear. No, gentlemen, Ned Blunt is not everybody. She expects me again tonight.

WILLMORE.

Egad, that's well; we'll all go.

BLUNT.

Not a soul! No, gentlemen, you are wits; I am a dull country rogue, I.   60

FREDERICK.

Well, sir, for all your person of quality, I shall be very glad to understand your purse be secure; 'tis our whole estate at present, which we are loath to hazard in one bottom. Come sir, unlade.

BLUNT.

Take the necessary trifle useless now to me, that am beloved   65 by such a gentlewoman. 'Adsheartlikins, money! Here, take mine too.

FREDERICK.

No, keep that to be cozened, that we may laugh.

WILLMORE.

Cozened? Death! Would I could meet with one that would cozen me of all the love I could spare tonight.   70

FREDERICK.

Pox, 'tis some common whore, upon my life.

49. any other] Q 1–3; another A, B.   64. unlade] Q 1–3; unload A, B.

---

63. *bottom*] ship's hold.
68. *cozened*] tricked, cheated.

BLUNT.

A whore? Yes, with such clothes, such jewels, such a house, such furniture, and so attended! A whore!

BELVILE.

Why yes, sir, they are whores, though they'll neither entertain you with drinking, swearing, or bawdry; are whores in   75
all those gay clothes and right jewels; are whores with those
great houses richly furnished with velvet beds, store of plate,
handsome attendance, and fine coaches; are whores, and
errant ones.

WILLMORE.

Pox on't, where do these fine whores live?   80

BELVILE.

Where no rogues in office, ycleped constables, dare give 'em
laws, nor the wine-inspired bullies of the town break their
windows; yet they are whores though this Essex calf believe
'em persons of quality.

BLUNT.

'Adsheartlikins, y'are all fools. There are things about this   85
Essex calf that shall take with the ladies, beyond all your
wit and parts. This shape and size, gentlemen, are not to be
despised; my waist, too, tolerably long, with other inviting
signs that shall be nameless.

WILLMORE.

Egad, I believe he may have met with some person of   90
quality that may be kind to him.

BELVILE.

Dost thou perceive any such tempting things about him
that should make a fine woman, and of quality, pick him
out from all mankind to throw away her youth and beauty
upon; nay, and her dear heart, too? No, no, Angellica has   95
raised the price too high.

76. with those] *Q1, Q3;* with   93. that] *Q1, Q3; om. Q2, A, B.*
Q2, A, B.

---

76. *right*] genuine.
77. *plate*] silver utensils.
79. *errant*] thorough.
81. *ycleped*] called.
83. *Essex calf*] fool, here also literally from Essex.

WILLMORE.

May she languish for mankind till she die, and be damned
for that one sin alone.

Enter two Bravos *and hang up a great picture of Angellica's against the
balcony, and two little ones at each side of the door.*

BELVILE.

See there the fair sign to the inn where a man may lodge
that's fool enough to give her price.   100
                              Willmore *gazes on the picture.*

BLUNT.

'Adsheartlikins, gentlemen, what's this?

BELVILE.

A famous courtesan, that's to be sold.

BLUNT.

How? To be sold? Nay, then I have nothing to say to her.
Sold? What impudence is practiced in this country; with
what order and decency whoring's established here by 105
virtue of the Inquisition! Come, let's be gone; I'm sure we're
no chapmen for this commodity.

FREDERICK.

Thou art none, I'm sure, unless thou couldst have her in
thy bed at a price of a coach in the street.

WILLMORE.

How wondrous fair she is! A thousand crowns a month? By 110
heaven, as many kingdoms were too little! A plague of this
poverty, of which I ne'er complain but when it hinders my
approach to beauty which virtue ne'er could purchase.
                                   Turns from the picture.

BLUNT.

What's this? (*Reads.*) "A thousand crowns a month"!
'Adsheartlikins, here's a sum! Sure 'tis a mistake. —[*To one* 115
of the Bravos.] Hark you, friend, does she take or give so
much by the month?

FREDERICK.

A thousand crowns! Why, 'tis a portion for the Infanta!

105. what] *Q1, Q3; om. Q2, A, B.*

---

118. *portion . . . Infanta*] dowry for the Spanish princess.

BLUNT.

Hark ye, friends, won't she trust?

BRAVO.

This is a trade, sir, that cannot live by credit.   120

Enter Don Pedro *in masquerade, followed by* Stephano.

BELVILE.

See, here's more company; let's walk off a while.

Exeunt English; Pedro *reads.*

PEDRO.

Fetch me a thousand crowns; I never wished to buy this
beauty at an easier rate.   *Passes off.*

Enter Angellica *and* Moretta *in the balcony, and draw a silk curtain.*

ANGELLICA.

Prithee, what said those fellows to thee?

BRAVO.

Madam, the first were admirers of beauty only, but no pur-   125
chasers; they were merry with your price and picture,
laughed at the sum, and so passed off.

ANGELLICA.

No matter, I'm not displeased with their rallying; their
wonder feeds my vanity, and he that wishes but to buy gives
me more pride than he that gives my price can make my   130
pleasure.

BRAVO.

Madam, the last I knew through all his disguises to be Don
Pedro, nephew to the general, and who was with him in
Pamplona.

ANGELLICA.

Don Pedro? My old gallant's nephew? When his uncle died   135
he left him a vast sum of money; it is he who was so in love
with me at Padua, and who used to make the general so
jealous.

MORETTA.

Is this he that used to prance before our window, and take

129. but] *Q1, Q3; om. Q2, A, B.*   130. make my] *Q1–3, A;* make me
B.

such care to show himself an amorous ass? If I am not 140
mistaken, he is the likeliest man to give your price.

ANGELLICA.

The man is brave and generous, but of a humor so uneasy
and inconstant that the victory over his heart is as soon lost as
won; a slave that can add little to the triumph of the conqueror. But inconstancy's the sin of all mankind, therefore 145
I'm resolved that nothing but gold shall charm my heart.

MORETTA.

I'm glad on't; 'tis only interest that women of our pro-
fession ought to consider, though I wonder what has kept
you from that general disease of our sex so long; I mean,
that of being in love.   150

ANGELLICA.

A kind but sullen star under which I had the happiness to be
born. Yet I have had no time for love; the bravest and
noblest of mankind have purchased my favors at so dear a
rate, as if no coin but gold were current with our trade. But
here's Don Pedro again; fetch me my lute, for 'tis for him or 155
Don Antonio the Viceroy's son that I have spread my nets.

Enter at one door Don Pedro, *Stephano*; Don Antonio *and* Diego [*his*
page] *at the other door, with people following him in masquerade, anticly*
attired, some with music. They both go up to the picture.

ANTONIO.

A thousand crowns! Had not the painter flattered her, I
should not think it dear.

PEDRO.

Flattered her? By heaven, he cannot. I have seen the original, nor is there one charm here more than adorns her face 160
and eyes; all this soft and sweet, with a certain languishing
air that no artist can represent.

ANTONIO.

What I heard of her beauty before had fired my soul, but
this confirmation of it has blown it to a flame.

PEDRO.

Ha!   165

164. to] *Q1, Q3; om. Q2;* into *A,*   165.] *Q1–3, A; S.P. and speech om. B.*
B.

PAGE.

Sir, I have known you throw away a thousand crowns on a worse face, and though y'are near your marriage, you may venture a little love here; Florinda will not miss it.

PEDRO (*aside*).

Ha! Florinda! Sure 'tis Antonio.

ANTONIO.

Florinda! Name not those distant joys; there's not one 170 thought of her will check my passion here.

PEDRO [*aside*].

Florinda scorned! (*A noise of a lute above.*) And all my hopes defeated of the possession of Angellica! (*Antonio gazes up.*) Her injuries, by heaven, he shall not boast of!

Song to a lute above.

SONG

[I]

When Damon first began to love   175
He languished in a soft desire,
And knew not how the gods to move,
  To lessen or increase his fire.
For Caelia in her charming eyes
Wore all love's sweets, and all his cruelties.   180

II

But as beneath a shade he lay,
Weaving of flowers for Caelia's hair,
She chanced to lead her flock that way,
And saw the am'rous shepherd there.
She gazed around upon the place,   185
And saw the grove, resembling night,
  To all the joys of love invite,
Whilst guilty smiles and blushes dressed her face.
At this the bashful youth all transport grew,
And with kind force he taught the virgin how   190
To yield what all his sighs could never do.

---

169. S.D. aside] *Q1, Q3*; om. *Q2,*
A, B.

170. Name not] *Q1, Q3, B*; Name
Q2, A.

180. sweets] *Q1, Q3*; sweet *Q2, A, B.*

Angellica *throws open the curtains and bows to* Antonio, *who pulls off his vizard and bows and blows up kisses.* Pedro, *unseen, looks in's face.* [*The curtains close.*]

ANTONIO.
By heaven, she's charming fair!
PEDRO (*aside*).
'Tis he, the false Antonio!
ANTONIO (*to the bravo*).
Friend, where must I pay my off'ring of love?
My thousand crowns I mean.   195
PEDRO.
That off'ring I have designed to make,
And yours will come too late.
ANTONIO.
Prithee begone; I shall grow angry else,
And then thou art not safe.
PEDRO.
My anger may be fatal, sir, as yours,   200
And he that enters here may prove this truth.
ANTONIO.
I know not who thou art, but I am sure thou'rt worth my
killing, for aiming at Angellica.   *They draw and fight.*

    Enter Willmore *and* Blunt, *who draw and part 'em.*

BLUNT.
'Adsheartlikins, here's fine doings.
WILLMORE.
Tilting for the wench, I'm sure. Nay, gad, if that would 205
win her I have as good a sword as the best of ye. Put up, put
up, and take another time and place, for this is designed for
lovers only.   *They all put up.*
PEDRO.
We are prevented; dare you meet me tomorrow on the Molo?
For I've a title to a better quarrel,   210
That of Florinda, in whose credulous heart
Thou'st made an int'rest, and destroyed my hopes.

191.1.] *Q 1–2; S.D. follows l. 193,*   197. too] *Q 1, Q 3, A, B;* not *Q 2.*
Q 3, A, B.   199. not] *Q 1, Q 3, A, B;* too *Q 2.*

209. *Molo*] mall.

ANTONIO.

Dare!

I'll meet thee there as early as the day.

PEDRO.

We will come thus disguised, that whosoever chance to get 215
the better, he may escape unknown.

ANTONIO.

It shall be so.   *Exeunt* Pedro *and* Stephano.

—Who should this rival be? Unless the English colonel, of
whom I've often heard Don Pedro speak. It must be he, and
time he were removed who lays a claim to all my happiness. 220

Willmore, *having gazed all this while on the picture, pulls down a little one.*

WILLMORE.

This posture's loose and negligent;
The sight on't would beget a warm desire
In souls whom impotence and age had chilled.
This must along with me.

BRAVO.

What means this rudeness, sir? Restore the picture.   225

ANTONIO.

Ha! Rudeness committed to the fair Angellica! —Restore
the picture, sir.

WILLMORE.

Indeed I will not, sir.

ANTONIO.

By heaven, but you shall.

WILLMORE.

Nay, do not show your sword; if you do, by this dear beauty, 230
I will show mine too.

ANTONIO.

What right can you pretend to't?

WILLMORE.

That of possession, which I will maintain. You, perhaps,
have a thousand crowns to give for the original.

ANTONIO.

No matter, sir, you shall restore the picture.   235

216. may] *Q1–2, A, B;* shall *Q3.*   220.1. *on*] *Q1–2, A, B; at Q3.*

[The curtains open;] Angellica *and* Moretta *above.*

ANGELLICA.
Oh, Moretta, what's the matter?
ANTONIO.
Or leave your life behind.
WILLMORE.
Death! You lie; I will do neither.

They fight. The Spaniards join with Antonio, Blunt *laying on like mad.*

ANGELLICA.
Hold, I command you, if for me you fight.
They leave off and bow.
WILLMORE *[aside].*
How heavenly fair she is! Ah, plague of her price!   240
ANGELLICA.
You sir, in buff, you that appear a soldier, that first began
this insolence—
WILLMORE.
'Tis true, I did so, if you call it insolence for a man to pre-
serve himself. I saw your charming picture and was
wounded; quite through my soul each pointed beauty ran; 245
and wanting a thousand crowns to procure my remedy, I
laid this little picture to my bosom, which, if you cannot
allow me, I'll resign.
ANGELLICA.
No, you may keep the trifle.
ANTONIO.
You shall first ask me leave, and this.   *Fight again as before.* 250

Enter Belvile *and* Frederick, *who join with the English.*

ANGELLICA.
Hold! Will you ruin me? —Biskey! Sebastian! Part 'em!
The Spaniards are beaten off.
MORETTA.
Oh, madam, we're undone. A pox upon that rude fellow;
he's set on to ruin us. We shall never see good days again
till all these fighting poor rogues are sent to the galleys.

235.1.] *Q2; S.D. follows l. 236, Q1,*   238.1.] *S.D. with l. 239.1, Q1–3, A,*
Q3, A, B.   *B.*

Enter Belvile, Blunt, Frederick, *and* Willmore *with's shirt bloody.*

BLUNT.

'Adsheartlikins, beat me at this sport and I'll ne'er wear 255
sword more.

BELVILE (*to* Willmore).

The devil's in thee for a mad fellow; thou art always one at
an unlucky adventure. Come, let's be gone whilst we're
safe, and remember these are Spaniards, a sort of people that
know how to revenge an affront.   260

FREDERICK.

You bleed! I hope you are not wounded.

WILLMORE.

Not much. A plague on your dons; if they fight no better
they'll ne'er recover Flanders. What the devil was't to them
that I took down the picture?

BLUNT.

Took it! 'Adsheartlikins, we'll have the great one too; 'tis 265
ours by conquest. Prithee help me up and I'll pull it down.

ANGELLICA [*to* Willmore].

Stay, sir, and ere you affront me farther let me know how
you durst commit this outrage. To you I speak, sir, for you
appear a gentleman.

WILLMORE.

To me, madam? —Gentlemen, your servant.   270

                                    Belvile *stays him.*

BELVILE.

Is the devil in thee? Dost know the danger of ent'ring the
house of an incensed courtesan?

WILLMORE.

I thank you for your care, but there are other matters in
hand, there are, though we have no great temptation.
Death! Let me go!   275

FREDERICK.

Yes, to your lodging if you will, but not in here. Damn these

254.1. *with's shirt*] *Q1; with shirts*   267. farther] *Q1, Q3;* further *Q2,*
Q2; with his shirt Q3; with their   *A, B.*
shirts A, B.   269. a] *Q1, Q3;* like a *Q2, A, B.*
262. on] *Q1, Q3;* upon *Q2, A, B.*   270. your] *Q1, Q3, A, B;* you *Q2.*

–40–

gay harlots; by this hand I'll have as sound and handsome
a whore for a patacoon. Death, man, she'll murder thee!

WILLMORE.

Oh, fear me not. Shall I not venture where a beauty calls?
A lovely charming beauty! For fear of danger? When, by 280
heaven, there's none so great as to long for her whilst I want
money to purchase her.

FREDERICK.

Therefore 'tis loss of time unless you had the thousand
crowns to pay.

WILLMORE.

It may be she may give a favor; at least I shall have the 285
pleasure of saluting her when I enter and when I depart.

BELVILE.

Pox, she'll as soon lie with thee as kiss thee, and sooner stab
than do either. You shall not go.

ANGELLICA.

Fear not, sir, all I have to wound with is my eyes.

BLUNT.

Let him go. 'Adsheartlikins, I believe the gentlewoman 290
means well.

BELVILE.

Well, take thy fortune; we'll expect you in the next street.
Farewell, fool, farewell.

WILLMORE.

'Bye, colonel.   *Goes in.*

FREDERICK.

The rogue's stark mad for a wench.   *Exeunt.* 295

[II.ii]   *A fine chamber.*
        Enter Willmore, Angellica, *and* Moretta.

ANGELLICA.

Insolent sir, how durst you pull down my picture?

WILLMORE.

Rather, how durst you set it up to tempt poor am'rous
mortals with so much excellence, which I find you have but

283. S.P. FREDERICK] *Q3, B;*
PEDRO *Q 1–2, A.*

---

278. *patacoon*] Portuguese or Spanish silver coin of nominal value.

too well consulted by the unmerciful price you set upon't.
Is all this heaven of beauty shown to move despair in those   5
that cannot buy? And can you think th'effects of that
despair should be less extravagant than I have shown?

ANGELLICA.

I sent for you to ask my pardon, sir, not to aggravate your
crime. I thought I should have seen you at my feet imploring
it.   10

WILLMORE.

You are deceived. I came to rail at you, and rail such
truths too, as shall let you see the vanity of that pride which
taught you how to set such price on sin.
For such it is whilst that which is love's due
Is meanly bartered for.   15

ANGELLICA.

Ha! Ha! Ha! Alas, good captain, what pity 'tis your
edifying doctrine will do no good upon me. Moretta, fetch
the gentleman a glass, and let him survey himself to see
what charms he has. —(*Aside, in a soft tone.*)   And guess my
business.   20

MORETTA.

He knows himself of old: I believe those breeches and he
have been acquainted ever since he was beaten at Worcester.

ANGELLICA.

Nay, do not abuse the poor creature.

MORETTA.

Good weatherbeaten corporal, will you march off? We have
no need of your doctrine, though you have of our charity.   25
But at present we have no scraps; we can afford no kindness
for God's sake. In fine, sirrah, the price is too high i'th'
mouth for you, therefore troop, I say.

WILLMORE.

Here, good forewoman of the shop, serve me and I'll be
gone.   30

11. and rail] *Q1-3;* and talk *A, B.*   28. mouth] *Q1, Q3;* month *Q2, A,*
13. such *Q1-3;* such a *A, B.*   *B.*
23. not] *Q1, Q3, A, B;* but *Q2.*

22. *Worcester*] site of the decisive defeat of Charles II by Cromwell,
September 3, 1651.
27–28. *high . . . mouth*] elevated.

MORETTA.

Keep it to pay your laundress; your linen stinks of the gun
room. For here's no selling by retail.

WILLMORE.

Thou hast sold plenty of thy stale ware at a cheap rate.

MORETTA.

Ay, the more silly kind heart I, but this is an age wherein
beauty is at higher rates. In fine, you know the price of this.   35

WILLMORE.

I grant you 'tis here set down, a thousand crowns a month.
Pray, how much may come to my share for a pistole?
Bawd, take your black lead and sum it up, that I may have
a pistole's worth of this vain gay thing, and I'll trouble you
no more.   40

MORETTA.

Pox on him, he'll fret me to death! Abominable fellow, I
tell thee we only sell by the whole piece.

WILLMORE.

'Tis very hard, the whole cargo or nothing. Faith, madam,
my stock will not reach it; I cannot be your chapman. Yet
I have countrymen in town, merchants of love like me; I'll   45
see if they'll put in for a share. We cannot lose much by it,
and what we have no use for, we'll sell upon the Friday's
mart at "Who gives more?" —I am studying, madam, how
to purchase you, though at present I am unprovided of
money.   50

ANGELLICA (aside).

Sure this from any other man would anger me; nor shall he
know the conquest he has made. —Poor angry man, how I
despise this railing.

WILLMORE.

Yes, I am poor. But I'm a gentleman,
And one that scorns this baseness which you practice.   55
Poor as I am I would not sell myself,

37. Pray ... pistole?] Q1, Q3; om.   39. this] Q1, Q3; these Q2, A, B.
Q2, A, B.   39. thing] Q3; things Q1–2, A, B.
39. pistole's] Q1, Q3; pistole Q2,
A, B.

---

37. pistole] Spanish gold coin worth about sixteen shillings.
47–48. upon ... more?"] at Friday's auction.

No, not to gain your charming high-prized person.
Though I admire you strangely for your beauty,
Yet I contemn your mind.
And yet I would at any rate enjoy you;   60
At your own rate; but cannot. See here
The only sum I can command on earth:
I know not where to eat when this is gone.
Yet such a slave I am to love and beauty
This last reserve I'll sacrifice to enjoy you.   65
Nay, do not frown, I know you're to be bought,
And would be bought by me. By me,
For a meaning trifling sum, if I could pay it down.
Which happy knowledge I will still repeat,
And lay it to my heart: it has a virtue in't,   70
And soon will cure those wounds your eyes have made.
And yet, there's something so divinely powerful there—
Nay, I will gaze, to let you see my strength.

> *Holds her, looks on her, and pauses and sighs.*

By heav'n, bright creature, I would not for the world
Thy fame were half so fair as is thy face.   75

> *Turns her away from him.*

ANGELLICA (*aside*).
　　His words go through me to the very soul.—
　　If you have nothing else to say to me—

WILLMORE.
　　Yes, you shall hear how infamous you are—
　　For which I do not hate thee—
　　But that secures my heart, and all the flames it feels   80
　　Are but so many lusts:
　　I know it by their sudden bold intrusion.
　　The fire's impatient and betrays; 'tis false.
　　For had it been the purer flame of love,
　　I should have pined and languished at your feet,   85
　　Ere found the impudence to have discovered it.
　　I now dare stand your scorn and your denial.

---

65. reserve] *Q1, Q3; om. Q2, A, B.*　71. cure] *Q1, Q3;* curse *Q2, A, B.*
67. By me,] *Q1–3, A; om. B.*　　75. is] *Q1, Q3, B; om. Q2, A.*

MORETTA.

    Sure she's bewitched, that she can stand thus tamely and
hear his saucy railing. —Sirrah, will you be gone?

ANGELLICA (*to* Moretta).

    How dare you take this liberty! Withdraw! —Pray tell me,   90
sir, are not you guilty of the same mercenary crime? When
a lady is proposed to you for a wife, you never ask how fair,
discreet, or virtuous she is, but what's her fortune; which,
if but small, you cry "She will not do my business," and
basely leave her, though she languish for you. Say, is not   95
this as poor?

WILLMORE.

    It is a barbarous custom, which I will scorn to defend in our
sex, and do despise in yours.

ANGELLICA.

    Thou'rt a brave fellow! Put up thy gold, and know,
    That were thy fortune as large as is thy soul,   100
    Thou shouldst not buy my love
    Couldst thou forget those mean effects of vanity
    Which set me out to sale,
    And as a lover prize my yielding joys.
    Canst thou believe they'll be entirely thine,   105
    Without considering they were mercenary?

WILLMORE.

    I cannot tell, I must bethink me first.
    (*Aside.*) Ha! Death, I'm going to believe her.

ANGELLICA.

    Prithee confirm that faith, or if thou canst not,
    Flatter me a little: 'twill please me from thy mouth.   110

WILLMORE (*aside*).

    Curse on thy charming tongue! Dost thou return
    My feigned contempt with so much subtlety?—
    Thou'st found the easiest way into my heart,
    Though I yet know that all thou say'st is false.

                                 Turning from her in rage.

ANGELLICA.

    By all that's good, 'tis real;   115

---

88. bewitched] *Q2–3, A, B;* be-   95. though] *Q2–3, A, B;* thou *Q1.*
witch *Q1.*   114.1. rage] *Q1–3; a rage A, B.*

I never loved before, though oft a mistress.
Shall my first vows be slighted?

WILLMORE (*aside*).

What can she mean?

ANGELLICA (*in an angry tone*).

I find you cannot credit me.

WILLMORE.

I know you take me for an errant ass,   120
An ass that may be soothed into belief,
And then be used at pleasure;
But, madam, I have been so often cheated
By perjured, soft, deluding hypocrites,
That I've no faith left for the cozening sex,   125
Especially for women of your trade.

ANGELLICA.

The low esteem you have of me perhaps
May bring my heart again:
For I have pride that yet surmounts my love.

                    She turns with pride; he holds her.

WILLMORE.

Throw off this pride, this enemy to bliss,   130
And show the power of love: 'tis with those arms
I can be only vanquished, made a slave.

ANGELLICA.

Is all my mighty expectation vanished?
No, I will not hear thee talk; thou hast a charm
In every word that draws my heart away,   135
And all the thousand trophies I designed
Thou hast undone. Why art thou soft?
Thy looks are bravely rough, and meant for war.
Couldst thou not storm on still?
I then perhaps had been as free as thou.   140

WILLMORE (*aside*).

Death, how she throws her fire about my soul!—
Take heed, fair creature, how you raise my hopes,
Which once assumed pretends to all dominion:
There's not a joy thou hast in store
I shall not then command.   145
For which I'll pay you back my soul, my life!
Come, let's begin th'account this happy minute!

-46-

ANGELLICA.

　　And will you pay me then the price I ask?

WILLMORE.

　　Oh, why dost thou draw me from an awful worship,
　　By showing thou art no divinity.   150
　　Conceal the fiend, and show me all the angel!
　　Keep me but ignorant, and I'll be devout
　　And pay my vows forever at this shrine.

Kneels and kisses her hand.

ANGELLICA.

　　The pay I mean is but thy love for mine.
　　Can you give that?   155

WILLMORE.

　　Entirely. Come, let's withdraw where I'll renew my vows,
　　and breathe 'em with such ardor thou shalt not doubt my
　　zeal.

ANGELLICA.

　　Thou hast a power too strong to be resisted.

Exeunt Willmore *and* Angellica.

MORETTA.

　　Now my curse go with you! Is all our project fallen to this? 160
　　To love the only enemy to our trade? Nay, to love such a
　　shameroon; a very beggar; nay, a pirate beggar, whose
　　business is to rifle and be gone; a no-purchase, no-pay
　　tatterdemalion, and English picaroon; a rogue that fights
　　for daily drink, and takes a pride in being loyally lousy? 165
　　Oh, I could curse now, if I durst. This is the fate of most
　　whores.

Trophies, which from believing fops we win,
Are spoils to those who cozen us again.   [*Exit.*]

The End of the Second Act.

164. and] *Q1–2;* an *Q3, A, B.*   169.1.] *Q1–2; om. Q3, A, B.*

149. *awful*] awe-inspiring.
162. *shameroon*] shameful person.
164. *picaroon*] rogue, pirate.

ACT III

A street.

Enter Florinda, Valeria, Hellena, *in antic different dresses from what they were in before;* Callis *attending.*

FLORINDA.

> I wonder what should make my brother in so ill a humor?
> I hope he has not found out our ramble this morning.

HELLENA.

> No, if he had, we should have heard on't at both ears, and
> have been mewed up this afternoon, which I would not for
> the world should have happened. Hey ho, I'm as sad as a   5
> lover's lute.

VALERIA.

> Well, methinks we have learnt this trade of gipsies as
> readily as if we had been bred upon the road to Loretto;
> and yet I did so fumble when I told the stranger his fortune
> that I was afraid I should have told my own and yours by   10
> mistake. But methinks Hellena has been very serious ever
> since.

FLORINDA.

> I would give my garters she were in love, to be revenged
> upon her for abusing me. How is't, Hellena?

HELLENA.

> Ah, would I had never seen my mad monsieur. And yet, for   15
> all your laughing, I am not in love. And yet this small
> acquaintance, o' my conscience, will never out of my head.

VALERIA.

> Ha! Ha! Ha! I laugh to think how thou art fitted with a
> lover, a fellow that I warrant loves every new face he sees.

HELLENA.

> Hum, he has not kept his word with me here, and may be   20
> \taken up. That thought is not very pleasant to me. What the
> deuce should this be now that I feel?

5. I'm as] *Q1-3;* I'm *A, B.*

0.2. *antic*] bizarre.
4. *mewed*] confined.
8. *Loretto*] town near Ancona, on the Adriatic.

VALERIA.

What is't like?

HELLENA.

Nay, the Lord knows, but if I should be hanged I cannot
choose but be angry and afraid when I think that mad   25
fellow should be in love with anybody but me. What to
think of myself I know not: would I could meet with some
true damned gipsy, that I might know my fortune.

VALERIA.

Know it! Why there's nothing so easy: thou wilt love this
wand'ring inconstant till thou find'st thyself hanged about   30
his neck, and then be as mad to get free again.'

FLORINDA.

Yes, Valeria, we shall see her bestride his baggage horse and
follow him to the campaign.

HELLENA.

So, so, now you are provided for there's no care taken of
poor me. But since you have set my heart a-wishing, I am   35
resolved to know for what; I will not die of the pip, so I will
not.

FLORINDA.

Art thou mad to talk so? Who will like thee well enough to
have thee, that hears what a mad wench thou art?

HELLENA.

Like me? I don't intend every he that likes me shall have   40
me, but he that I like. I should have stayed in the nunnery
still if I had liked my lady abbess as well as she liked me. No,
I came thence not, as my wise brother imagines, to take an
eternal farewell of the world, but to love and to be beloved;
and I will be beloved, or I'll get one of your men, so I will.   45

VALERIA.

Am I put into the number of lovers?

HELLENA.

You? Why, coz, I know thou'rt too good-natured to leave
us in any design; thou wouldst venture a cast though thou

43. thence not] *Q1–2, A, B;* not   48. wouldst] wou't *Q1–2;* would
thence *Q3.*   *Q3;* won't *A, B.*
47. Why] *Q1–3;* My *A, B.*

---

36. *the pip*] slight ailment or fit of peevish behavior.
48. *venture a cast*] try a throw of the dice.

comest off a loser, especially with such a gamester. I
observed your man, and your willing ear incline that way; 50
and if you are not a lover, 'tis an art soon learnt—that I
find.   *Sighs.*

FLORINDA.

I wonder how you learnt to love so easily. I had a thousand
charms to meet my eyes and ears ere I could yield, and
'twas the knowledge of Belvile's merit, not the surprising 55
person, took my soul. Thou art too rash, to give a heart at
first sight.

HELLENA.

Hang your considering lover! I never thought beyond the
fancy that 'twas a very pretty, idle, silly kind of pleasure to
pass one's time with: to write little soft nonsensical billets, 60
and with great difficulty and danger receive answers in
which I shall have my beauty praised, my wit admired,
though little or none, and have the vanity and power to
know I am desirable. Then I have the more inclination that
way because I am to be a nun, and so shall not be suspected 65
to have any such earthly thoughts about me; but when I
walk thus—and sigh thus—they'll think my mind's upon my
monastery, and cry, "How happy 'tis she's so resolved." But
not a word of man.

FLORINDA.

What a mad creature's this!   70

HELLENA.

I'll warrant, if my brother hears either of you sigh, he
cries gravely, "I fear you have the indiscretion to be in
love, but take heed of the honor of our house, and your
own unspotted fame"; and so he conjures on till he has
laid the soft winged god in your hearts, or broke the bird's 75
nest. But see, here comes your lover, but where's my
inconstant? Let's step aside, and we may learn something.
                                                                      Go aside.

Enter Belvile, Frederick, *and* Blunt.

50. observed] *Q3, A, B;* observe   50. ear] *Q1, Q3;* ears *Q2, A, B.*
Q1–2.   69. a] *Q2–3, A, B; om. Q1.*

75–76. *laid . . . nest*] destroyed your feeling or his opportunity. Possibly
from the proverb "Destroy the nests and the birds will fly away."

BELVILE.

What means this! The picture's taken in.

BLUNT.

It may be the wench is good-natured, and will be kind
gratis. Your friend's a proper handsome fellow.   80

BELVILE.

I rather think she has cut his throat and is fled; I am mad
he should throw himself into dangers. Pox on't, I shall want
him, too, at night. Let's knock and ask for him.

HELLENA.

My heart goes a-pit, a-pat, for fear 'tis my man they talk of.

Knock; Moretta *above.*

MORETTA.

What would you have?   85

BELVILE.

Tell the stranger that entered here about two hours ago that
his friends stay here for him.

MORETTA.

A curse upon him for Moretta: would he were at the devil!
But he's coming to you.

Enter Willmore.

HELLENA.

Ay, ay 'tis he. Oh, how this vexes me!   90

BELVILE.

And how and how, dear lad, has fortune smiled? Are we to
break her windows, or raise up altars to her, hah?

WILLMORE.

Does not my fortune sit triumphant on my brow? Dost not
see the little wanton god there all gay and smiling? Have I
not an air about my face and eyes that distinguish me from   95
the crowd of common lovers? By heaven, Cupid's quiver
has not half so many darts as her eyes! Oh, such a *bona roba!*
To sleep in her arms is lying *in fresco,* all perfumed air about
me.

83. too, at night] *Q1, Q3;* tonight   86. ago] *Q1–3, A;* go *B.*
Q2, A, B.   89.1.] *Q3; om. Q1–2, A, B.*

97. *bona roba*] courtesan.
98. *in fresco*] in cool refreshing air.

-51-

HELLENA (*aside*).

Here's fine encouragement for me to fool on!   100

WILLMORE.

Hark'ee, where didst thou purchase that rich Canary we
drank today? Tell me, that I may adore the spigot and
sacrifice to the butt. The juice was divine; into which I must
dip my rosary, and then bless all things that I would have
bold or fortunate.   105

BELVILE.

Well, sir, let's go take a bottle and hear the story of your
success.

FREDERICK.

Would not French wine do better?

WILLMORE.

Damn the hungry balderdash! Cheerful sack has a generous
virtue in't inspiring a successful confidence, gives eloquence 110
to the tongue and vigor to the soul, and has in a few hours
completed all my hopes and wishes! There's nothing left to
raise a new desire in me. Come, let's be gay and wanton.
And, gentlemen, study; study what you want, for here are
friends that will supply gentlemen. [*Jingles gold.*] Hark 115
what a charming sound they make! 'Tis he and she gold
whilst here, and shall beget new pleasures every moment.

BLUNT.

But hark'ee, sir, you are not married, are you?

WILLMORE.

All the honey of matrimony but none of the sting, friend.

BLUNT.

'Adsheartlikins, thou'rt a fortunate rogue!   120

WILLMORE.

I am so, sir: let these inform you! Ha, how sweetly they
chime! Pox of poverty: it makes a man a slave, makes wit
and honor sneak. My soul grew lean and rusty for want of
credit.

116. he and she] *B;* he and the   117. and] *Q1–3; om. A, B.*
Q1–2, A; the he and the she *Q3.*

---

101. *Canary*] sweet wine made on the Canary Islands.
109. hungry *balderdash*] worthless mixture of liquors.

BLUNT.

'Adsheartlikins, this I like well; it looks like my lucky 125
bargain! Oh, how I long for the approach of my squire, that
is to conduct me to her house again. Why, here's two provided for!

FREDERICK.

By this light, y'are happy men.

BLUNT.

Fortune is pleased to smile on us, gentlemen, to smile on us. 130

Enter Sancho *and pulls down* Blunt *by the sleeve; they go aside.*

SANCHO.

Sir, my lady expects you. She has removed all that might
oppose your will and pleasure, and is impatient till you
come.

BLUNT.

Sir, I'll attend you. —Oh the happiest rogue! I'll take no
leave, lest they either dog me or stay me.   135

Exit with Sancho.

BELVILE.

But then the little gipsy is forgot?

WILLMORE.

A mischief on thee for putting her into my thoughts! I had
quite forgot her else, and this night's debauch had drunk her
quite down.

HELLENA.

Had it so, good captain!   *Claps him on the back.* 140

WILLMORE (*aside*).

Ha! I hope she did not hear me!

HELLENA.

What, afraid of such a champion?

WILLMORE.

Oh, you're a fine lady of your word, are you not? To make
a man languish a whole day—

HELLENA.

In tedious search of me.   145

130.1. *down*] *Q1–2; om. Q3, A, B.*   141. me] *Q1–3; om. A, B.*

---

135. *dog me*] follow me.

WILLMORE.

Egad, child, thou'rt in the right. Hadst thou seen what a
melancholy dog I have been ever since I was a lover, how I
have walked the streets like a Capuchin, with my hands in
my sleeves—faith, sweetheart, thou wouldst pity me.

HELLENA [aside].

Now if I should be hanged I can't be angry with him, he 150
dissembles so heartily. —Alas, good captain, what pains you
have taken; now were I ungrateful not to reward so true a
servant.

WILLMORE.

Poor soul, that's kindly said; I see thou barest a conscience.
Come then, for a beginning show me thy dear face.   155

HELLENA.

I'm afraid, my small acquaintance, you have been staying
that swinging stomach you boasted of this morning. I then
remember my little collation would have gone down with
you without the sauce of a handsome face. Is your stomach
so queasy now?   160

WILLMORE.

Faith, long fasting, child, spoils a man's appetite. Yet if you
durst treat, I could so lay about me still—

HELLENA.

And would you fall to before a priest says grace?

WILLMORE.

Oh fie, fie, what an old out-of-fashioned thing hast thou
named? Thou couldst not dash me more out of countenance 165
shouldst thou show me an ugly face.

Whilst he is seemingly courting Hellena, *enter* Angellica, Moretta, Biskey,
and Sebastian, *all in masquerade.* Angellica *sees* Willmore *and stares.*

ANGELLICA.

Heavens, 'tis he! And passionately fond to see another
woman!

MORETTA.

What could you less expect from such a swaggerer?

154. barest] *Q1–3*; bearest *A, B.*   167. 'tis] *Q3*; 'ts *Q1*; it's *Q2*; is't
163. to] *Q1–2, A, B*; too *Q3.*   *A, B.*
166.2. stares] *Q1–3*; starts *A, B.*

---

148. *Capuchin*] austere monastic of an order established in 1528.
158. *collation*] light meal.

ANGELLICA.

Expect? As much as I paid him: a heart entire,   170
Which I had pride enough to think when'er I gave,
It would have raised the man above the vulgar,
Made him all soul, and that all soft and constant.

HELLENA.

You see, captain, how willing I am to be friends with you,
till time and ill luck make us lovers; and ask you the ques- 175
tion first rather than put your modesty to the blush by
asking me. For alas, I know you captains are such strict
men, and such severe observers of your vows to chastity,
that 'twill be hard to prevail with your tender conscience
to marry a young willing maid.   180

WILLMORE.

Do not abuse me, for fear I should take thee at thy word
and marry thee indeed, which I'm sure will be revenge
sufficient.

HELLENA.

O' my conscience, that will be our destiny, because we are
both of one humor: I am as inconstant as you, for I have 185
considered, captain, that a handsome woman has a great
deal to do whilst her face is good. For then is our harvest-
time to gather friends, and should I in these days of my
youth catch a fit of foolish constancy, I were undone: 'tis
loitering by daylight in our great journey. Therefore, I 190
declare I'll allow but one year for love, one year for indif-
ference, and one year for hate; and then go hang yourself,
for I profess myself the gay, the kind, and the inconstant.
The devil's in't if this won't please you!

WILLMORE.

Oh, most damnably. I have a heart with a hole quite 195
through it too; no prison mine, to keep a mistress in.

ANGELLICA (aside).

Perjured man! How I believe thee now!

HELLENA.

Well, I see our business as well as humors are alike: yours to
cozen as many maids as will trust you, and I as many men

178. and such] *Q1, Q3; om. Q2, A,*   184. O'] *Q1–3, B;* Oh *A.*
B.   190. I] *Q1, Q3; om. Q2, A, B.*

as have faith. See if I have not as desperate a lying look as 200
you can have for the heart of you. (*Pulls off her vizard; he
starts.*) How do you like it, captain?

WILLMORE.

Like it! By heaven, I never saw so much beauty! Oh, the
charms of those sprightly black eyes! That strangely fair
face, full of smiles and dimples! Those soft round melting 205
cherry lips and small even white teeth! Not to be expressed,
but silently adored! [*She replaces her mask.*] Oh, one look
more, and strike me dumb, or I shall repeat nothing else till
I'm mad.

He seems to court her to pull off her vizard; she refuses.

ANGELLICA.

I can endure no more. Nor is it fit to interrupt him, for if I 210
do, my jealousy has so destroyed my reason I shall undo
him. Therefore I'll retire, and you, Sebastian (*to one of her
bravos*), follow that woman and learn who 'tis; while you
(*to the other bravo*) tell the fugitive I would speak to him
instantly.   *Exit.* 215

This while Florinda *is talking to* Belvile, *who stands sullenly;* Frederick
courting Valeria.

VALERIA [*to* Belvile].

Prithee, dear stranger, be not so sullen, for though you have
lost your love you see my friend frankly offers you hers to
play with in the meantime.

BELVILE.

Faith, madam, I am sorry I can't play at her game.

FREDERICK [*to* Valeria].

Pray leave your intercession and mind your own affair. 220
They'll better agree apart: he's a modest sigher in company,
but alone no woman 'scapes him.

FLORINDA [*aside*].

Sure he does but rally. Yet, if it should be true? I'll tempt
him farther. —Believe me, noble stranger, I'm no common
mistress. And for a little proof on't, wear this jewel. Nay, 225

223. rally] *Q 1–3, A;* railly *B.*

_____

225. *jewel*] costly ornament; here probably a locket.

take it, sir, 'tis right, and bills of exchange may sometimes
miscarry.

BELVILE.

Madam, why am I chose out of all mankind to be the object
of your bounty?

VALERIA.

There's another civil question asked.   230

FREDERICK [*aside*].

Pox of's modesty; it spoils his own markets and hinders
mine.

FLORINDA.

Sir, from my window I have often seen you, and women of
my quality have so few opportunities for love that we ought
to lose none.   235

FREDERICK [*to* Valeria].

Ay, this is something! Here's a woman! When shall I be
blest with so much kindness from your fair mouth? —(*Aside
to* Belvile.)   Take the jewel, fool!

BELVILE.

You tempt me strangely, madam, every way—

FLORINDA (*aside*).

So, if I find him false, my whole repose is gone.   240

BELVILE.

And but for a vow I've made to a very fair lady, this goodness had subdued me.

FREDERICK [*aside to* Belvile].

Pox on't, be kind, in pity to me be kind. For I am to thrive
here but as you treat her friend.

HELLENA.

Tell me what you did in yonder house, and I'll unmask.   245

WILLMORE.

Yonder house? Oh, I went to a—to—why, there's a friend
of mine lives there.

HELLENA.

What, a she or a he friend?

234. my] *Q 1, Q3; om.Q2, A, B.*   241. fair] *Q3; om. Q2, A, and some
copies of Q1;* fine *B.*

226. *bills of exchange*] orders on a foreign agent directing the payment of
money.

WILLMORE.

>A man, upon honor, a man. A she friend? No, no, madam, you have done my business, I thank you.   250

HELLENA.

>And was't your man friend that had more darts in's eyes than Cupid carries in's whole budget of arrows?

WILLMORE.

>So—

HELLENA.

>"Ah, such a *bona roba*! To be in her arms is lying *in fresco*, all perfumed air about me." Was this your man friend too?   255

WILLMORE.

>So—

HELLENA.

>That gave you the he and the she gold, that begets young pleasures?

WILLMORE.

>Well, well, madam, then you can see there are ladies in the world that will not be cruel. There are, madam, there are. 260

HELLENA.

>And there be men, too, as fine, wild, inconstant fellows as yourself. There be, captain, there be, if you go to that now. Therefore, I'm resolved—

WILLMORE.

>Oh!

HELLENA.

>To see your face no more—   265

WILLMORE.

>Oh!

HELLENA.

>Till tomorrow.

WILLMORE.

>Egad, you frighted me.

HELLENA.

>Nor then neither, unless you'll swear never to see that lady more.   270

WILLMORE.

>See her! Why, never to think of womankind again.

---

252. *budget*] quiver.

HELLENA.

    Kneel, and swear.   *Kneels; she gives him her hand.*

WILLMORE.

    I do, never to think, to see, to love, nor lie, with any but
thyself.

HELLENA.

    Kiss the book.   275

WILLMORE.

    Oh, most religiously.   *Kisses her hand.*

HELLENA.

    Now what a wicked creature am I, to damn a proper fellow.

CALLIS (*to* Florinda).

    Madam, I'll stay no longer: 'tis e'en dark.

FLORINDA [*to* Belvile].

    However, sir, I'll leave this with you, that when I'm gone
you may repent the opportunity you have lost by your 280
modesty.

    Gives him the jewel, which is her picture, and exit. He gazes after her.

WILLMORE [*to* Hellena].

    'Twill be an age till tomorrow, and till then I will most
impatiently expect you. Adieu, my dear pretty angel.

                                   Exeunt all the women.

BELVILE.

    Ha! Florinda's picture! 'Twas she herself. What a dull dog
was I! I would have given the world for one minute's dis- 285
course with her.

FREDERICK.

    This comes of your modesty. Ah, pox o' your vow; 'twas ten
to one but we had lost the jewel by't.

BELVILE.

    Willmore, the blessed'st opportunity lost! Florinda, friends,
Florinda!   290

WILLMORE.

    Ah, rogue! Such black eyes! Such a face! Such a mouth!
Such teeth! And so much wit!

BELVILE.

    All, all, and a thousand charms besides.

WILLMORE.

    Why, dost thou know her?

BEVILE.

Know her! Ay, ay, and a pox take me with all my heart for 295
being so modest.

WILLMORE.

But hark'ee, friend of mine, are you my rival? And have I
been only beating the bush all this while?

BELVILE.

I understand thee not. I'm mad! See here—   *Shows the picture.*

WILLMORE.

Ha! Whose picture's this? 'Tis a fine wench!   300

FREDERICK.

The colonel's mistress, sir.

WILLMORE.

Oh, oh, here.   (*Gives the picture back.*)   I thought't had been
another prize. Come, come, a bottle will set thee right
again.

BELVILE.

I am content to try, and by that time 'twill be late enough 305
for our design.

WILLMORE.

Agreed.

> *Love does all day the soul's great empire keep,*
> *But wine at night lulls the soft god asleep.*   *Exeunt.*

[III.ii]   *Lucetta's house.*
                Enter Blunt *and* Lucetta *with a light.*

LUCETTA.

Now we are safe and free: no fears of the coming home of
my old jealous husband, which made me a little thoughtful
when you came in first. But now love is all the business of
my soul.

BLUNT.

I am transported! —(*Aside.*)   Pox on't, that I had but some   5
fine things to say to her, such as lovers use. I was a fool
not to learn of Fred a little by heart before I came. Something I must say. —'Adsheartlikins, sweet soul, I am not
used to compliment, but I'm an honest gentleman, and thy
humble servant.   10

309. S.D.] *Q1–3, A; om. B.*

LUCETTA.

I have nothing to pay for so great a favor, but such a love as
cannot but be great, since at first sight of that sweet face and
shape it made me your absolute captive.

BLUNT (*aside*).

Kind heart, how prettily she talks! Egad, I'll show her
husband a Spanish trick: send him out of the world and   15
marry her; she's damnably in love with me, and will ne'er
mind settlements, and so there's that saved.

LUCETTA.

Well, sir, I'll go and undress me, and be with you instantly.

BLUNT.

Make haste then, for 'adsheartlikins, dear soul, thou canst
not guess at the pain of a longing lover when his joys are   20
drawn within the compass of a few minutes.

LUCETTA.

You speak my sense, and I'll make haste to prove it.   *Exit.*

BLUNT.

'Tis a rare girl, and this one night's enjoyment with her will
be worth all the days I ever passed in Essex. Would she
would go with me into England, though to say truth, there's   25
plenty of whores already. Put a box on 'em, they are such
mercenary prodigal whores that they want such a one as
this, that's free and generous, to give 'em good examples.
Why, what a house she has, how rich and fine!

Enter Sancho.

SANCHO.

Sir, my lady has sent me to conduct you to her chamber.   30

BLUNT.

Sir, I shall be proud to follow. —(*Aside.*)   Here's one of her
servants too; 'adsheartlikins, by this garb and gravity he
might be a justice of peace in Essex, and is but a pimp here.

Exeunt.

22. prove] *Q1, Q3;* provide *Q2, A,*   29.1. *Enter*] *Q1, Q3; Exit Q2, A, B.*
B, which give speech as aside.   *All texts place S.D. after l. 30.*
23. S.D.] *Q1, Q3; om. Q2, A, B.*   33.1. S.D. *Exeunt] Q1–3, A; Exit B.*

17. *settlements*] antenuptial dispositions of property for the benefit of the
wife.
34. *justice of peace*] an official of considerable importance in the seventeenth century.

[III.iii]

*The scene changes to a chamber with an alcove bed in't, a table, etc.; Lucetta
in bed. Enter Sancho and Blunt, who takes the candle of Sancho at the door.*

SANCHO.

    Sir, my commission reaches no farther.

BLUNT.

    Sir, I'll excuse your compliment.   [*Exit* Sancho.]
    —What, in bed, my sweet mistress?

LUCETTA.

    You see, I still outdo you in kindness.

BLUNT.

    And thou shalt see what haste I'll make to quit scores. Oh,   5
    the luckiest rogue!   *He undresses himself.*

LUCETTA.

    Should you be false or cruel now—

BLUNT.

    False! 'Adsheartlikins, what dost thou take me for, a Jew?
    An insensible heathen? A pox of thy old jealous husband:
    an he were dead, egad, sweet soul, it should be none of my   10
    fault if I did not marry thee.

LUCETTA.

    It never should be mine.

BLUNT.

    Good soul! I'm the fortunatest dog!

LUCETTA.

    Are you not undressed yet?

BLUNT.

    As much as my impatience will permit.   15
              Goes toward the bed in his shirt, drawers, etc.

LUCETTA.

    Hold, sir, put out the light; it may betray us else.

BLUNT.

    Anything; I need no other light but that of thine eyes. —
    (*Aside.*) 'Adsheartlikins, there I think I had it.

    Puts out the candle; the bed descends; he gropes about to find it.

---

6. S.D. *He*] *Q1, Q3; om. Q2, A, B.*   15.1. *shirt . . . etc.*] *Q1 (some copies),*
8. a] *Q1, Q3, B; om. Q2, A.*   *Q3; shirt, drawers. Q2, and some copies
                                    of Q1; shirt and drawers. A, B.*

Why, why, where am I got? What, not yet? Where are you,
sweetest? —Ah, the rogue's silent now. A pretty love-trick   20
this; how she'll laugh at me anon! —You need not, my dear
rogue, you need not! I'm all on fire already; come, come,
now call me, in pity. —Sure I'm enchanted! I have been
round the chamber, and can find neither woman nor bed.
I locked the door; I'm sure she cannot go that way, or if she   25
could, the bed could not. —Enough, enough, my pretty
wanton; do not carry the jest too far! (*Lights on a trap, and
is let down.*)   —Ha! Betrayed! Dogs! Rogues! Pimps! Help!
Help!

Enter Lucetta, Phillipo, *and* Sancho *with a light.*

PHILLIPO.

Ha! Ha! Ha! He's dispatched finely.   30
LUCETTA.

Now, sir, had I been coy, we had missed of this booty.
PHILLIPO.

Nay, when I saw 'twas a substantial fool, I was mollified.
But when you dote upon a serenading coxcomb, upon a
face, fine clothes, and a lute, it makes me rage.
LUCETTA.

You know I was never guilty of that folly, my dear Phillipo,   35
but with yourself. But come, let's see what we have got by this.
PHILLIPO.

A rich coat; sword and hat; these breeches, too, are well
lined! See here, a gold watch! A purse— Ha! Gold! At
least two hundred pistoles! A bunch of diamond rings, and
one with the family arms! A gold box, with a medal of his   40
king, and his lady mother's picture! These were sacred relics,
believe me. See, the waistband of his breeches have a mine
of gold—old queen Bess's! We have a quarrel to her ever
since eighty-eight, and may therefore justify the theft: the
Inquisition might have committed it.   45

22. on] *Q1–3;* on a *A, B.*   35. was never] *Q1, Q3;* never was
28. Pimps!] *Q1, Q3;* Imps! *Q2, A,*   *Q2, A, B.*
B.

44. *eighty-eight*] The Spanish Armada was destroyed in 1588, during
Queen Elizabeth's reign.

LUCETTA.

See, a bracelet of bowed gold! These his sisters tied about
his arm at parting. But well, for all this, I fear his being a
stranger may make a noise and hinder our trade with them
hereafter.

PHILLIPO.

That's our security: he is not only a stranger to us, but to   50
the country too. The common shore into which he is
descended, thou know'st, conducts him into another street,
which this light will hinder him from ever finding again.
He knows neither your name, nor that of the street where
your house is; nay, nor the way to his own lodgings.   55

LUCETTA.

And art thou not an unmerciful rogue, not to afford him one
night for all this? I should not have been such a Jew.

PHILLIPO.

Blame me not, Lucetta, to keep as much of thee as I can to
myself. Come, that thought makes me wanton; let's to bed.
—Sancho, lock up these.   60

> This is the fleece which fools do bear,
> Designed for witty men to shear.   Exeunt.

[III.iv]

The scene changes, and discovers Blunt *creeping out of a common shore; his
face, etc., all dirty.*

BLUNT (*climbing up*).

Oh, Lord, I am got out at last, and, which is a miracle,
without a clue. And now to damning and cursing! But if that
would ease me, where shall I begin? With my fortune,
myself, or the quean that cozened me? What a dog was I to
believe in woman! Oh, coxcomb! Ignorant conceited   5

46. sisters] *Q1, Q3;* sister *Q2, A, B.*   62. *shear*] *Q1; share Q2–3, A, B.*
54. that of] *Q1, Q3;* that *Q2, A;*   [III.iv]
om. B.   4. quean] *Q1–3, B;* queen *A.*
58. me] *Q1, Q3, B; om. Q2, A.*   5. woman] *Q1–3;* women *A, B.*

46. *bowed*] bent, curved.
51. *shore*] sewer.
[III.iv]
4. *quean*] slut.

coxcomb! To fancy she could be enamored with my person!
At first sight enamored! Oh, I'm a cursed puppy! 'Tis plain,
fool was writ upon my forehead! She perceived it; saw the
Essex calf there. For what allurements could there be in this
countenance, which I can endure because I'm acquainted   10
with it. Oh dull, silly dog, to be thus soothed into a cozening!
Had I been drunk, I might fondly have credited the young
quean; but as I was in my right wits to be thus cheated,
confirms it: I am a dull believing English country fop. But
my comrades! Death and the devil, there's the worst of all!   15
Then a ballad will be sung tomorrow on the Prado, to a
lousy tune of the enchanted squire and the annihilated
damsel. But Fred—that rogue—and the colonel will abuse me
beyond all Christian patience. Had she left me my clothes,
I have a bill of exchange at home would have saved my   20
credit. But now all hope is taken from me. Well, I'll home,
if I can find the way, with this consolation: that I am not
the first kind believing coxcomb; but there are, gallants,
many such good natures amongst ye.

   And though you've better arts to hide your follies, 25
   'Adsheartlikins, y'are all as errant cullies. *Exit.*

[III.v]   *Scene, the garden in the night.*
  Enter Florinda *in an undress, with a key and a little box.*

FLORINDA.

 Well, thus far I'm in my way to happiness. I have got
myself free from Callis; my brother too, I find by yonder
light, is got into his cabinet, and thinks not of me; I have
by good fortune got the key of the garden back door. I'll
open it to prevent Belvile's knocking: a little noise will now   5
alarm my brother. Now am I as fearful as a young thief.
(*Unlocks the door.*) Hark! What noise is that? Oh, 'twas the
wind that played amongst the boughs. Belvile stays long,

[III.iv]   14. confirms it: I] *Q1, Q3;* con-
7. At] *Q1, Q3;* At the *Q2, A, B.* firms I *Q2, A, B.*
           26. S.D.] *Q3; om. Q1-2, A, B.*

16. *Prado*] fashionable promenade.
26. *cullies*] dupes.
[III.v]
 3. *cabinet*] private room.

methinks; it's time. Stay, for fear of a surprise, I'll hide
these jewels in yonder jasmine. *She goes to lay down the box.* 10

Enter Willmore, *drunk.*

WILLMORE.

What the devil is become of these fellows Belvile and
Frederick? They promised to stay at the next corner for me,
but who the devil knows the corner of a full moon? Now,
whereabouts am I? Ha, what have we here? A garden! A
very convenient place to sleep in. Ha! What has God sent us 15
here? A female! By this light, a woman! I'm a dog if it be
not a very wench!

FLORINDA.

He's come! Ha! Who's there?

WILLMORE.

Sweet soul, let me salute thy shoestring.

FLORINDA [*aside*].

'Tis not my Belvile. Good heavens, I know him not! —Who 20
are you, and from whence come you?

WILLMORE.

Prithee, prithee, child, not so many hard questions! Let it
suffice I am here, child. Come, come kiss me.

FLORINDA.

Good gods! What luck is mine?

WILLMORE.

Only good luck, child, parlous good luck. Come hither. 25
—'Tis a delicate shining wench. By this hand, she's perfumed, and smells like any nosegay. —Prithee, dear soul,
let's not play the fool and lose time—precious time. For as
Gad shall save me, I'm as honest a fellow as breathes, though
I'm a little disguised at present. Come, I say. Why, thou 30
mayst be free with me: I'll be very secret. I'll not boast who
'twas obliged me, not I; for hang me if I know thy name.

FLORINDA.

Heavens! What a filthy beast is this!

WILLMORE.

I am so, and thou ought'st the sooner to lie with me for
that reason. For look you, child, there will be no sin in't, 35

25. *parlous*] exceedingly.
30. *disguised*] drunk.

because 'twas neither designed nor premeditated: 'tis pure
accident on both sides. That's a certain thing now. Indeed,
should I make love to you, and you vow fidelity, and swear
and lie till you believed and yielded—that were to make it
wilful fornication, the crying sin of the nation. Thou art,   40
therefore, as thou art a good Christian, obliged in conscience
to deny me nothing. Now, come be kind without any
more idle prating.

FLORINDA.

Oh, I am ruined! Wicked man, unhand me!

WILLMORE.

Wicked? Egad, child, a judge, were he young and vigorous,   45
and saw those eyes of thine, would know 'twas they gave
the first blow, the first provocation. Come, prithee let's lose
no time, I say. This is a fine convenient place.

FLORINDA.

Sir, let me go, I conjure you, or I'll call out.

WILLMORE.

Ay, ay, you were best to call witness to see how finely you   50
treat me. Do!

FLORINDA.

I'll cry murder, rape, or anything, if you do not instantly let
me go!

WILLMORE.

A rape! Come, come, you lie, you baggage, you lie. What!
I'll warrant you would fain have the world believe now that   55
you are not so forward as I. No, not you. Why at this time
of night was your cobweb door set open, dear spider, but to
catch flies? Ha! Come, or I shall be damnably angry. Why,
what a coil is here!

FLORINDA.

Sir, can you think—   60

WILLMORE.

That you would do't for nothing? Oh, oh, I find what you
would be at. Look here, here's a pistole for you. Here's a
work indeed! Here, take it, I say!

39–40. that . . . nation] *Q1–3; om.*
A, B.

---

59. *coil*] difficulty, tumult.

FLORINDA.

For heaven's sake, sir, as you're a gentleman—

WILLMORE.

So now, now, she would be wheedling me for more! What, 65
you will not take it then? You are resolved you will not?
Come, come, take it or I'll put it up again, for look ye, I
never give more. Why, how now, mistress, are you so high
i'th' mouth a pistole won't down with you? Ha! Why, what
a work's here! In good time! Come, no struggling to be gone. 70
But an y'are good at a dumb wrestle, I'm for ye. Look ye,
I'm for ye.   *She struggles with him.*

Enter Belvile *and* Frederick.

BELVILE.

The door is open. A pox of this mad fellow! I'm angry that
we've lost him; I durst have sworn he had followed us.

FREDERICK.

But you were so hasty, colonel, to be gone.   75

FLORINDA.

Help! Help! Murder! Help! Oh, I am ruined!

BELVILE.

Ha! Sure that's Florinda's voice! (*Comes up to them.*)   A
man! —Villain, let go that lady!

A noise; Willmore *turns and draws;* Frederick *interposes.*

FLORINDA.

Belvile! Heavens! My brother too is coming, and 'twill be
impossible to escape. Belvile, I conjure you to walk under 80
my chamber window, from whence I'll give you some
instructions what to do. This rude man has undone us.   *Exit.*

WILLMORE.

Belvile!

Enter Pedro, Stephano, *and other servants, with lights.*

PEDRO.

I'm betrayed! Run, Stephano, and see if Florinda be safe.
                                      Exit Stephano.

They fight, and Pedro's *party beats 'em out.*

—So, whoe'er they be, all is not well. I'll to Florinda's 85
chamber.   *Going out, meets* Stephano.

70. to] *Q1, Q3; om. Q2, A, B.*

STEPHANO.

> You need not, sir: the poor lady's fast asleep, and thinks no
> harm. I would not awake her, sir, for fear of frighting her
> with your danger.

PEDRO.

> I'm glad she's there. —Rascals, how came the garden door   90
> open?

STEPHANO.

> That question comes too late, sir. Some of my fellow servants
> masquerading, I'll warrant.

PEDRO.

> Masquerading! A lewd custom to debauch our youth!
> There's something more in this than I imagine.   *Exeunt.* 95

[III.vi]   *Scene changes to the street.*
Enter Belvile *in rage,* Frederick *holding him,* Willmore *melancholy.*

WILLMORE.

> Why, how the devil should I know Florinda?

BELVILE.

> Ah, plague of your ignorance! If it had not been Florinda,
> must you be a beast? A brute? A senseless swine?

WILLMORE.

> Well, sir, you see I am endued with patience: I can bear.
> Though egad, y'are very free with me, methinks. I was in   5
> good hopes the quarrel would have been on my side, for so
> uncivilly interrupting me.

BELVILE.

> Peace, brute, whilst thou'rt safe. Oh, I'm distracted!

WILLMORE.

> Nay, nay, I'm an unlucky dog, that's certain.

BELVILE.

> Ah, curse upon the star that ruled my birth, or whatsoever   10
> other influence that makes me still so wretched.

WILLMORE.

> Thou break'st my heart with these complaints. There is no
> star in fault, no influence but sack, the cursed sack I drunk.

88. awake] *Q1–2, A, B;* wake *Q3.*   13. drunk] *Q1, Q3;* drank *Q2, A,*
[III.vi]   *B.*
3. swine] *Q1, Q3, A, B;* swines *Q2.*

FREDERICK.

Why, how the devil came you so drunk?

WILLMORE.

Why, how the devil came you so sober?   15

BELVILE.

A curse upon his thin skull, he was always beforehand that
way.

FREDERICK.

Prithee, dear colonel, forgive him; he's sorry for his fault.

BELVILE.

He's always so after he has done a mischief. A plague on all
such brutes!   20

WILLMORE.

By this light, I took her for an errant harlot.

BELVILE.

Damn your debauched opinion! Tell me, sot, hadst thou so
much sense and light about thee to distinguish her woman,
and couldst not see something about her face and person to
strike an awful reverence into thy soul?   25

WILLMORE.

Faith no, I considered her as mere a woman as I could
wish.

BELVILE.

'Sdeath, I have no patience. Draw, or I'll kill you!

WILLMORE.

Let that alone till tomorrow, and if I set not all right again,
use your pleasure.   30

BELVILE.

Tomorrow! Damn it,
The spiteful light will lead me to no happiness.
Tomorrow is Antonio's, and perhaps
Guides him to my undoing. Oh, that I could meet
This rival, this powerful fortunate!   35

WILLMORE.

What then?

BELVILE.

Let thy own reason, or my rage, instruct thee.

24. couldst] *Q1-2, A, B;* couldst
thou *Q3.*

WILLMORE.

    I shall be finely informed then, no doubt. Hear me, colonel,
hear me; show me the man and I'll do his business.

BELVILE.

    I know him no more than thou, or if I did I should not need   40
thy aid.

WILLMORE.

    This you say is Angellica's house; I promised the kind
baggage to lie with her tonight.   *Offers to go in.*

    Enter Antonio *and his* Page. Antonio *knocks on the hilt of's sword.*

ANTONIO.

    You paid the thousand crowns I directed?

PAGE.

    To the lady's old woman, sir, I did.   45

WILLMORE.

    Who the devil have we here?

BELVILE.

    I'll now plant myself under Florinda's window, and if I find
no comfort there, I'll die.   *Exeunt* Belvile *and* Frederick.

          Enter Moretta.

MORETTA.

    Page?

PAGE.

    Here's my lord.   50

WILLMORE.

    How is this? A picaroon going to board my frigate? —Here's
one chase gun for you!

Drawing his sword, justles Antonio, *who turns and draws. They fight;*
Antonio *falls.*

MORETTA.

    Oh, bless us! We're all undone!   *Runs in and shuts the door.*

PAGE.

    Help! Murder!

          Belvile *returns at the noise of fighting.*

---

52. *chase gun*] bow or stern gun used in pursuit.

BELVILE.

    Ha! The mad rogue's engaged in some unlucky adventure   55
again.

Enter two or three Masqueraders.

MASQUERADER.

    Ha! A man killed!

WILLMORE.

    How, a man killed? Then I'll go home to sleep.

            Puts up and reels out. Exeunt Masqueraders *another way.*

BELVILE.

    Who should it be? Pray heaven the rogue is safe, for all my
quarrel to him.   60

As Belvile *is groping about, enter an* Officer *and six* Soldiers.

SOLDIER.

    Who's there?

OFFICER.

    So, here's one dispatched. Secure the murderer.

BELVILE.

    Do not mistake my charity for murder! I came to his
assistance!   *Soldiers sieze on* Belvile.

OFFICER.

    That shall be tried, sir. St. Jago! Swords drawn in the   65
Carnival time!   *Goes to* Antonio.

ANTONIO.

    Thy hand, prithee.

OFFICER.

    Ha! Don Antonio! Look well to the villain there. —How
is it, sir?

ANTONIO.

    I'm hurt.   70

BELVILE.

    Has my humanity made me a criminal?

OFFICER.

    Away with him!

BELVILE.

    What a curst chance is this!   *Exeunt soldiers with* Belvile.

ANTONIO [*aside*].

This is the man that has set upon me twice. —(*To the officer.*) Carry him to my apartment till you have farther 75
orders from me.   *Exit* Antonio, *led.*

The End of the Third Act.

74–75. S.D.] *printed with 76.* S.D., 76.1.] *Q 1–2; om. Q 3, A, B.*
Q 1–3, A, B.

ACT IV

[IV.i]   *A fine room.*
                  Discovers Belvile *as by dark alone.*

BELVILE.

When shall I be weary of railing on fortune, who is resolved
never to turn with smiles upon me? Two such defeats in one
night none but the devil and that mad rogue could have
contrived to have plagued me with. I am here a prisoner.
But where, heaven knows. And if there be murder done, I   5
can soon decide the fate of a stranger in a nation without
mercy. Yet this is nothing to the torture my soul bows with
when I think of losing my fair, my dear Florinda. Hark, my
door opens. A light! A man, and seems of quality. Armed,
too! Now shall I die like a dog, without defense.   10

Enter Antonio *in a nightgown, with a light; his arm in a scarf, and a sword*
under his arm. He sets the candle on the table.

ANTONIO.

Sir, I come to know what injuries I have done you, that
could provoke you to so mean an action as to attack me
basely without allowing time for my defense?

BELVILE.

Sir, for a man in my circumstances to plead innocence
would look like fear. But view me well, and you will find no   15
marks of coward on me, nor anything that betrays that
brutality you accuse me with.

ANTONIO.

In vain, sir, you impose upon my sense. You are not only he
who drew on me last night, but yesterday before the same
house, that of Angellica. Yet there is something in your face   20
and mien that makes me wish I were mistaken.

BELVILE.

I own I fought today in the defense of a friend of mine with
whom you, if you're the same, and your party were first
engaged. Perhaps you think this crime enough to kill me,
but if you do, I cannot fear you'll do it basely.   25

16. coward] *Q1, Q3;* a coward   21. that . . . mistaken] *Q1, Q3;*
Q2, A, B.   *om. Q2, A, B.*

ANTONIO.

No sir, I'll make you fit for a defense with this.

Gives him the sword.

BELVILE.

This gallantry surprises me, nor know I how to use this present, sir, against a man so brave.

ANTONIO.

You shall not need. For know, I come to snatch you from a danger that is decreed against you: perhaps your life, or 30 long imprisonment. And 'twas with so much courage you offended, I cannot see you punished.

BELVILE.

How shall I pay this generosity?

ANTONIO.

It had been safer to have killed another than have attempted me. To show your danger, sir, I'll let you know my quality: 35 and 'tis the Viceroy's son whom you have wounded.

BELVILE.

The Viceroy's son! —(*Aside.*)   Death and confusion! Was this plague reserved to complete all the rest? Obliged by him, the man of all the world I would destroy!

ANTONIO.

You seem disordered, sir. 40

BELVILE.

Yes, trust me, I am, and 'tis with pain that man receives such bounties who wants the power to pay 'em back again.

ANTONIO.

To gallant spirits 'tis indeed uneasy, but you may quickly overpay me, sir.

BELVILE (*aside*).

Then I am well. Kind heaven, but set us even, that I may 45 fight with him and keep my honor safe. —Oh, I'm impatient, sir, to be discounting the mighty debt I owe you. Command me quickly.

ANTONIO.

I have a quarrel with a rival, sir, about the maid we love.

BELVILE (*aside*).

Death, 'tis Florinda he means! That thought destroys my 50 reason, and I shall kill him.

---

35. *quality*] rank.
47. *discounting*] reducing.

ANTONIO.

My rival, sir, is one has all the virtues man can boast of—

BELVILE (*aside*).

Death, who should this be?

ANTONIO.

He challenged me to meet him on the Molo as soon as day
appeared, but last night's quarrel has made my arm unfit   55
to guide a sword.

BELVILE.

I apprehend you, sir. You'd have me kill the man that lays
a claim to the maid you speak of. I'll do't. I'll fly to do't!

ANTONIO.

Sir, do you know her?

BELVILE.

No, sir, but 'tis enough she is admired by you.   60

ANTONIO.

Sir, I shall rob you of the glory on't, for you must fight
under my name and dress.

BELVILE.

That opinion must be strangely obliging that makes you
think I can personate the brave Antonio, whom I can but
strive to imitate.   65

ANTONIO

You say too much to my advantage. Come, sir, the day
appears that calls you forth. Within, sir, is the habit.

Exit Antonio.

BELVILE.

Fantastic fortune, thou deceitful light,
That cheats the wearied traveler by night,
Though on a precipice each step you tread,   70
I am resolved to follow where you lead.   *Exit.*

[IV.ii]   *The Molo.*

Enter Florinda *and* Callis *in masks, with* Stephano.

FLORINDA (*aside*).

I'm dying with my fears: Belvile's not coming as I expected

---

54. S.P. ANTONIO] *Q3, B; om.*   69. wearied] *Q1, Q3, B;* wearier
Q1-2, A.   *Q2, A.*

under my window makes me believe that all those fears are
true. —Canst thou not tell with whom my brother fights?

STEPHANO.

No, madam, they were both in masquerade. I was by when
they challenged one another, and they had decided the   5
quarrel then, but were prevented by some cavaliers; which
made 'em put it off till now. But I am sure 'tis about you
they fight.

FLORINDA (aside).

Nay, then, 'tis with Belvile, for what other lover have I that
dares fight for me except Antonio, and he is too much in   10
favor with my brother. If it be he, for whom shall I direct
my prayers to heaven?

STEPHANO.

Madam, I must leave you, for if my master see me, I shall
be hanged for being your conductor. I escaped narrowly
for the excuse I made for you last night i'th' garden.   15

FLORINDA.

And I'll reward thee for't. Prithee, no more.   *Exit* Stephano.

Enter Don Pedro *in his masking habit.*

PEDRO.

Antonio's late today; the place will fill, and we may be
prevented.   *Walks about.*

FLORINDA (aside).

Antonio? Sure I heard amiss.

PEDRO.

But who will not excuse a happy lover   20
When soft fair arms confine the yielding neck,
And the kind whisper languishingly breathes
"Must you be gone so soon?"
Sure I had dwelt forever on her bosom—
But stay, he's here.   25

Enter Bevile *dressed in Antonio's clothes.*

FLORINDA [aside].

'Tis not Belvile; half my fears are vanished.

---

5. had] *Q1, Q3, A, B; om. Q2.*   14. I] *B; om. Q1-3, A.*
9. S.D. *aside*] *Q1, Q3; om. Q2, A,*   16.1. *masking*] *Q1-3; mask, A, B.*
B.

PEDRO.

Antonio!

BELVILE (*aside*).

This must be he. —You're early, sir; I do not use to be outdone this way.

PEDRO.

The wretched, sir, are watchful, and 'tis enough you've the   30
advantage of me in Angellica.

BELVILE (*aside*).

Angellica! Or I've mistook my man, or else Antonio! Can he forget his interest in Florinda and fight for common prize?

PEDRO.

Come, sir, you know our terms.   35

BELVILE (*aside*).

By heaven, not I. —No talking; I am ready, sir.

Offers to fight; Florinda *runs in.*

FLORINDA (*to* Belvile).

Oh, hold! Whoe'er you be, I do conjure you hold! If you strike here, I die!

PEDRO.

Florinda!

BELVILE.

Florinda imploring for my rival!   40

PEDRO.

Away; this kindness is unseasonable.

Puts her by; they fight; she runs in just as Belvile *disarms* Pedro.

FLORINDA.

Who are you, sir, that dares deny my prayers?

BELVILE.

Thy prayers destroy him; if thou wouldst preserve him, do that thou'rt unacquainted with, and curse him.

She holds him.

FLORINDA.

By all you hold most dear, by her you love,   45
I do conjure you, touch him not.

37–38. If . . . die!] *Q1–3; om. A, B.*   42. dares] *Q1, Q3;* dare *Q2, A, B.*

32. *Or . . . or*] either . . . or.

BELVILE.

By her I love?
See, I obey, and at your feet resign
The useless trophy of my victory.

Lays his sword at her feet.

PEDRO.

Antonio, you've done enough to prove you love Florinda.   50

BELVILE.

Love Florinda! Does heaven love adoration, prayer, or
penitence? Love her? Here, sir, your sword again.

Snatches up the sword and gives it to him.

Upon this truth I'll fight my life away.

PEDRO.

No, you've redeemed my sister, and my friendship.

He gives him Florinda, *and pulls off his vizard to show his face, and puts it
on again.*

BELVILE.

Don Pedro!   55

PEDRO.

Can you resign your claims to other women, and give your
heart entirely to Florinda?

BELVILE.

Entire, as dying saints' confessions are!
I can delay my happiness no longer:
This minute let me make Florinda mine.   60

PEDRO.

This minute let it be. No time so proper: this night my
father will arrive from Rome, and possibly may hinder what
we purpose.

FLORINDA.

Oh, heavens! This minute?

Enter masqueraders and pass over.

BELVILE.

Oh, do not ruin me!   65

PEDRO.

The place begins to fill, and that we may not be observed,

do you walk off to St. Peter's church, where I will meet you
and conclude your happiness.

BELVILE.

I'll meet you there. —(*Aside.*)　If there be no more saints'
churches in Naples.　　　　　　　　　　　　　　　　　70

FLORINDA.

Oh, stay, sir, and recall your hasty doom!
Alas, I have not yet prepared my heart
To entertain so strange a guest.

PEDRO.

Away; this silly modesty is assumed too late.

BELVILE.

Heaven, madam, what do you do?　　　　　　　　　　　75

FLORINDA.

Do? Despise the man that lays a tyrant's claim
To what he ought to conquer by submission.

BELVILE.

You do not know me. Move a little this way.　　*Draws her aside.*

FLORINDA.

Yes, you may force me even to the altar,
But not the holy man that offers there　　　　　　　　80
Shall force me to be thine.

　　　　　　　　　　　　　Pedro *talks to* Callis *this while.*

BELVILE.

Oh, do not lose so blest an opportunity!

　　　　　　　　　　　　　　　　Pulls off his vizard.

See, 'tis your Belvile, not Antonio,
Whom your mistaken scorn and anger ruins.

FLORINDA.

Belvile!　　　　　　　　　　　　　　　　　　　　85
Where was my soul it could not meet thy voice,
And take this knowledge in.

As they are talking, enter Willmore, *finely dressed, and* Frederick.

WILLMORE.

No intelligence? No news of Belvile yet? Well, I am the
most unlucky rascal in nature. Ha! Am I deceived, or is it

68. your] *Q1, Q3, A, B;* you *Q2.*　　force me *Q2, A, B.*
79. force me even] *Q1, Q3;* even　　87.1. *are*] *Q1–3, B; were A.*

he? Look, Fred! 'Tis he, my dear Belvile!   90

Runs and embraces him; Belvile's vizard falls out on's hand.

BELVILE.
Hell and confusion seize thee!

PEDRO.
Ha! Belvile! I beg your pardon, sir.   *Takes* Florinda *from him.*

BELVILE.
Nay, touch her not. She's mine by conquest, sir;
I won her by my sword.

WILLMORE.
Didst thou so? And egad, child, we'll keep her by the sword.   95

Draws on Pedro; Belvile *goes between.*

BELVILE.
Stand off!
Thou'rt so profanely lewd, so curst by heaven,
All quarrels thou espousest must be fatal.

WILLMORE.
Nay, an you be so hot, my valor's coy,
And shall be courted when you want it next.   100

Puts up his sword.

BELVILE (*to* Pedro).
You know I ought to claim a victor's right,
But you're the brother to divine Florinda,
To whom I'm such a slave. To purchase her
I durst not hurt the man she holds so dear.

PEDRO.
'Twas by Antonio's, not by Belvile's sword   105
This question should have been decided, sir.
I must confess much to your bravery's due,
Both now and when I met you last in arms;
But I am nicely punctual in my word,
As men of honor ought, and beg your pardon: 110
For this mistake another time shall clear.

Aside to Florinda *as they are going out.*

90. Fred!] *Q1, Q3; as S.P. in Q2,*   90.1. *Runs . . . hand.*] *Q1, Q3;*
A, B, with following sentence assigned   *Vizard . . . hand; runs . . . him.* Bel-
to him.   vile's *Q2; Vizard . . . hand; runs . . .*
                                             him. A, B.

111. *clear*] make up.

—This was some plot between you and Belvile,
But I'll prevent you.   [*Exeunt* Pedro *and* Florinda.]

Belvile *looks after her and begins to walk up and down in rage.*

WILLMORE.

Do not be modest now and lose the woman. But if we shall
fetch her back so—   115
BELVILE.

Do not speak to me!
WILLMORE.

Not speak to you? Egad, I'll speak to you, and will be
answered, too.
BELVILE.

Will you, sir?
WILLMORE.

I know I've done some mischief, but I'm so dull a puppy 120
that I'm the son of a whore if I know how or where. Prithee
inform my understanding.
BELVILE.

Leave me, I say, and leave me instantly!
WILLMORE.

I will not leave you in this humor, nor till I know my crime.
BELVILE.

Death, I'll tell you, sir—   125

Draws and runs at Willmore; *he runs out,* Belvile *after him;* Frederick
interposes.

Enter Angellica, Moretta, *and* Sebastian.

ANGELLICA.

Ha! Sebastian, is that not Willmore? Haste! haste and
bring him back.   [*Exit* Sebastian.]
FREDERICK [*aside*].

The colonel's mad: I never saw him thus before. I'll after
'em lest he do some mischief, for I am sure Willmore will
not draw on him.   *Exit.* 130
ANGELLICA.

I am all rage! My first desires defeated!
For one for aught he knows that has no

113.1. *rage*] *Q1–3; a rage A, B.*   131. all] *Q1–2, A, B; om. Q3.*

Other merit than her quality,
Her being Don Pedro's sister. He loves her!
I know 'tis so. Dull, dull, insensible,   135
He will not see me now, though oft invited,
And broke his word last night. False perjured man!
He that but yesterday fought for my favors,
And would have made his life a sacrifice
To've gained one night with me,   140
Must now be hired and courted to my arms.

MORETTA.

I told you what would come on't, but Moretta's an old
doting fool. Why did you give him five hundred crowns, but
to set himself out for other lovers? You should have kept him
poor if you had meant to have had any good from him.   145

ANGELLICA.

Oh, name not such mean trifles! Had I given
Him all my youth has earned from sin,
I had not lost a thought nor sigh upon't.
But I have given him my eternal rest,
My whole repose, my future joys, my heart!   150
My virgin heart, Moretta! Oh, 'tis gone!

MORETTA.

Curse on him, here he comes. How fine she has made him,
too.

Enter Willmore *and* Sebastian; Angellica *turns and walks away.*

WILLMORE.

How now, turned shadow?
Fly when I pursue, and follow when I fly?   *Sings.* 155
        Stay, gentle shadow of my dove,
            And tell me ere I go,
        Whether the substance may not prove
            A fleeting thing like you.
                                As she turns she looks on him.
There's a soft kind look remaining yet.   160

147. Him all] *with l. 146*, *Q1–3*, *A*,   153.1. Willmore *and* Sebastian; An-
B.   gellica] *Q1*, *Q3*, *A*, *B*; Willmore,
                                           Sebastian *and* Angellica *Q2*.

ANGELLICA.

Well, sir, you may be gay: all happiness, all joys pursue you
still. Fortune's your slave, and gives you every hour choice
of new hearts and beauties, till you are cloyed with the
repeated bliss which others vainly languish for. But know,
false man, that I shall be revenged.   *Turns away in rage.* 165

WILLMORE.

So, gad, there are of those faint-hearted lovers, whom such
a sharp lesson next their hearts would make as impotent as
fourscore. Pox o' this whining; my business is to laugh and
love. A pox on't, I hate your sullen lover: a man shall lose
as much time to put you in humor now as would serve to 170
gain a new woman.

ANGELLICA.

I scorn to cool that fire I cannot raise,
Or do the drudgery of your virtuous mistress.

WILLMORE.

A virtuous mistress? Death, what a thing thou hast found
out for me! Why, what the devil should I do with a virtuous 175
woman, a sort of ill-natured creatures that take a pride to tor-
ment a lover. Virtue is but an infirmity in woman, a disease
that renders even the handsome ungrateful; whilst the ill-
favored, for want of solicitations and address, only fancy
themselves so. I have lain with a woman of quality who has 180
all the while been railing at whores.

ANGELLICA.

I will not answer for your mistress's virtue,
Though she be young enough to know no guilt;
And I could wish you would persuade my heart
'Twas the two hundred thousand crowns you courted.   185

WILLMORE.

Two hundred thousand crowns! What story's this? What
trick? What woman, ha?

ANGELLICA.

How strange you make it. Have you forgot the creature you
entertained on the Piazzo last night?

WILLMORE (*aside*).

Ha! My gipsy worth two hundred thousand crowns! Oh, 190
how I long to be with her! Pox, I knew she was of quality.

176. take] *Q1, Q3, A, B;* takes *Q2.*

ANGELLICA.

False man! I see my ruin in thy face.

How many vows you breathed upon my bosom

Never to be unjust. Have you forgot so soon?

WILLMORE.

Faith, no; I was just coming to repeat 'em. But here's a   195
humor indeed would make a man a saint. —(*Aside.*)   Would
she would be angry enough to leave me, and command me
not to wait on her.

Enter Hellena *dressed in man's clothes.*

HELLENA.

This must be Angellica: I know it by her mumping matron
here. Ay, ay, 'tis she. My mad captain's with her, too, for all   200
his swearing. How this unconstant humor makes me love
him! —Pray, good grave gentlewoman, is not this Angellica?

MORETTA.

My too young sir, it is. —[*Aside.*]   I hope 'tis one from Don
Antonio.   *Goes to* Angellica.

HELLENA (*aside*).

Well, something I'll do to vex him for this.   205

ANGELLICA.

I will not speak with him. Am I in humor to receive a
lover?

WILLMORE.

Not speak with him? Why, I'll be gone, and wait your idler
minutes. Can I show less obedience to the thing I love so
fondly?   *Offers to go.* 210

ANGELLICA.

A fine excuse this! Stay—

WILLMORE.

And hinder your advantage? Should I repay your bounties
so ungratefully?

ANGELLICA [*to* Hellena].

Come hither, boy.   —[*To* Willmore.]   That I may let you
see

How much above the advantages you name   215

I prize one minute's joy with you.

201. unconstant] *Q1, Q3;* inconstant *Q2, A, B.*

---

199. *mumping*] sullen.

WILLMORE (*impatient to be gone*).

> Oh, you destroy me with this endearment. —[*Aside.*] Death,
> how shall I get away? —Madam, 'twill not be fit I should
> be seen with you. Besides, it will not be convenient. And
> I've a friend—that's dangerously sick.   220

ANGELLICA.

> I see you're impatient. Yet you shall stay.

WILLMORE (*aside*).

> And miss my assignation with my gipsy.

Walks about impatiently; Moretta *brings* Hellena, *who addresses herself to*
Angellica.

HELLENA.

> Madam,
> You'll hardly pardon my instrusion
> When you shall know my business,   225
> And I'm too young to tell my tale with art;
> But there must be a wondrous store of goodness
> Where so much beauty dwells.

ANGELLICA.

> A pretty advocate, whoever sent thee.
> Prithee proceed.
>
> > *To* Willmore, *who is stealing off.*
> —Nay, sir, you shall not go.   230

WILLMORE (*aside*).

> Then I shall lose my dear gipsy forever. Pox on't, she stays
> me out of spite.

HELLENA.

> I am related to a lady, madam,
> Young, rich, and nobly born, but has the fate
> To be in love with a young English gentleman.   235
> Strangely she loves him, at first sight she loved him,
> But did adore him when she heard him speak;
> For he, she said, had charms in every word
> That failed not to surprise, to wound and conquer.

WILLMORE (*aside*).

> Ha! Egad, I hope this concerns me.   240

ANGELLICA (*aside*).

> 'Tis my false man he means. Would he were gone:
> This praise will raise his pride, and ruin me.
>
> > (*To* Willmore.) —Well,

Since you are so impatient to be gone,
I will release you, sir.

WILLMORE (*aside*).

Nay, then I'm sure 'twas me he spoke of: this cannot be the 245
effects of kindness in her. —No, Madam, I've considered
better on't, and will not give you cause of jealousy.

ANGELLICA.

But sir, I've business that—

WILLMORE.

This shall not do; I know 'tis but to try me.

ANGELLICA.

Well, to your story, boy. —(*Aside*). Though 'twill undo 250
me.

HELLENA.

With this addition to his other beauties,
He won her unresisting tender heart.
He vowed, and sighed, and swore he loved her dearly;
And she believed the cunning flatterer,   255
And thought herself the happiest maid alive.
Today was the appointed time by both
To consummate their bliss:
The virgin, altar, and the priest were dressed;
And whilst she languished for th'expected bridegroom,   260
She heard he paid his broken vows to you.

WILLMORE (*aside*).

So, this is some dear rogue that's in love with me, and this
way lets me know it. Or, if it be not me, he means someone
whose place I may supply.

ANGELLICA.

Now I perceive   265
The cause of thy impatience to be gone,
And all the business of this glorious dress.

WILLMORE.

Damn the young prater; I know not what he means.

HELLENA.

Madam,
In your fair eyes I read too much concern   270
To tell my farther business.

---

258. their] *Q1-2, A, B;* the *Q3.*   263. he] *Q3;* she *Q1-2, A, B.*
262. S.D. *aside*] *B; om. Q1-3, A.*

ANGELLICA.

Prithee, sweet youth, talk on: thou mayst perhaps
Raise here a storm that may undo my passion,
And then I'll grant thee anything.

HELLENA.

Madam, 'tis to entreat you (oh unreasonable)   275
You would not see this stranger.
For if you do, she vows you are undone;
Though nature never made a man so excellent,
And sure he 'ad been a god, but for inconstancy.

WILLMORE (*aside*).

Ah, rogue, how finely he's instructed! 'Tis plain, some 280
woman that has seen me *en passant*.

ANGELLICA.

Oh, I shall burst with jealousy! Do you know the man you
speak of?

HELLENA.

Yes, madam, he used to be in buff and scarlet.

ANGELLICA (*to* Willmore).

Thou false as hell, what canst thou say to this?   285

WILLMORE.

By heaven—

ANGELLICA.

Hold, do not damn thyself—

HELLENA.

Nor hope to be believed.   *He walks about; they follow.*

ANGELLICA.

Oh perjured man!
Is't thus you pay my generous passion back?   290

HELLENA.

Why would you, sir, abuse my lady's faith?

ANGELLICA.

And use me so unhumanely.

HELLENA.

A maid so young, so innocent—

WILLMORE.

Ah, young devil!

280. S.D. *aside*] *Q1–2, A, B; om.*   292. unhumanely] *Q1;* inhumanely
Q3.   *Q2–3, A, B.*

ANGELLICA.

Dost thou not know thy life is in my power?   295

HELLENA.

Or think my lady cannot be revenged?

WILLMORE (*aside*).

So, so, the storm comes finely on.

ANGELLICA.

Now thou art silent: guilt has struck thee dumb.

Oh, hadst thou still been so, I'd lived in safety.

> *She turns away and weeps.*

WILLMORE (*aside* to Hellena).

Sweetheart, the lady's name and house—quickly! I'm   300
impatient to be with her.

Looks toward Angellica *to watch her turning, and as she comes towards them
he meets her.*

HELLENA (*aside*).

So, now is he for another woman.

WILLMORE.

The impudent'st young thing in nature: I cannot persuade
him out of his error, madam.

ANGELLICA.

I know he's in the right; yet thou'st a tongue   305
That would persuade him to deny his faith.

> *In rage walks away.*

WILLMORE (*said softly to* Hellena).

Her name, her name, dear boy!

HELLENA.

Have you forgot it, sir?

WILLMORE (*aside*).

Oh, I perceive he's not to know I am a stranger to his lady.
—Yes, yes, I do know, but I have forgot the—   (Angellica 310
turns.) —By heaven, such early confidence I never saw.

ANGELLICA.

Did I not charge you with this mistress, sir?
Which you denied, though I beheld your perjury.
This little generosity of thine has rendered back my heart.

> *Walks away.*

295. in] *Q2-3, A, B; om. Q1.*   307. S.D. *said*] *Q1-2, A, B; om.*
                                        Q3.

WILLMORE (*to* Hellena).

So, you have made sweet work here, my little mischief. Look 315
your lady be kind and good-natured now, or I shall have but
a cursed bargain on't.   (Angellica *turns toward them*.) —The
rogue's bred up to mischief; art thou so great a fool to credit
him?

ANGELLICA.

Yes, I do, and you in vain impose upon me. Come hither, 320
boy. Is not this he you spake of?

HELLENA.

I think it is. I cannot swear, but I vow he has just such
another lying lover's look.

Hellena *looks in his face; he gazes on her.*

WILLMORE (*aside*).

Ha! Do I not know that face? By heaven, my little gipsy!
What a dull dog was I: had I but looked that way I'd 325
known her. Are all my hopes of a new woman banished?
—Egad, if I do not fit thee for this, hang me. —[*To* Angellica.]   Madam, I have found out the plot.

HELLENA [*aside*].

Oh lord, what does he say? Am I discovered now?

WILLMORE.

Do you see this young spark here?   330

HELLENA [*aside*].

He'll tell her who I am.

WILLMORE.

Who do you think this is?

HELLENA [*aside*].

Ay, ay, he does know me. —Nay, dear captain, I am
undone if you discover me.

WILLMORE.

Nay, nay, no cogging; she shall know what a precious 335
mistress I have.

HELLENA.

Will you be such a devil?

321. spake] *Q1;* speak *Q2–3, A, B.*

_____

335. *cogging*] wheedling.

WILLMORE.

Nay, nay, I'll teach you to spoil sport you will not make.
—This small ambassador comes not from a person of
quality, as you imagine and he says, but from a very errant 340
gipsy: the talking'st, prating'st, canting'st little animal thou
ever saw'st.

ANGELLICA.

What news you tell me, that's the thing I mean.

HELLENA (*aside*).

Would I were well off the place! If ever I go a-captain-
hunting again—   345

WILLMORE.

Mean that thing? That gipsy thing? Thou mayst as well be
jealous of thy monkey or parrot as of her. A German motion
were worth a dozen of her, and a dream were a better enjoyment—a creature of a constitution fitter for heaven than
man.   350

HELLENA (*aside*).

Though I'm sure he lies, yet this vexes me.

ANGELLICA.

You are mistaken: she's a Spanish woman made up of no
such dull materials.

WILLMORE.

Materials? Egad, an she be made of any that will either
dispense or admit of love, I'll be bound to continence.   355

HELLENA (*aside to him*).

Unreasonable man, do you think so?

WILLMORE.

You may return, my little brazen head, and tell your lady,
that till she be handsome enough to be beloved, or I dull
enough to be religious, there will be small hopes of me.

ANGELLICA.

Did you not promise, then, to marry her?   360

WILLMORE.

Not I, by heaven.

---

348. of her] *Q1, Q3;* her *Q2, A, B.*   357. S.P. WILLMORE] *Q3, A, B;*
355. continence] *Q1, Q3;* con-   *om. Q1-2.*
tinuance *Q2, A, B.*   357. tell] *Q1, Q3, A, B;* tell to *Q2.*

347. *motion*] puppet show.

ANGELLICA.

You cannot undeceive my fears and torments, till you have
vowed you will not marry her.

HELLENA (*aside*).

If he swears that, he'll be revenged on me indeed for all my
rogueries.   365

ANGELLICA.

I know what arguments you'll bring against me: fortune and
honor.

WILLMORE.

Honor! I tell you, I hate it in your sex; and those that fancy
themselves possessed of that foppery are the most imperti-
nently troublesome of all womankind, and will transgress   370
nine commandments to keep one. And to satisfy your
jealousy, I swear—

HELLENA (*aside to him*).

Oh, no swearing, dear captain.

WILLMORE.

If it were possible I should ever be inclined to marry, it
should be some kind young sinner: one that has generosity   375
enough to give a favor handsomely to one that can ask it
discreetly, one that has wit enough to manage an intrigue of
love. Oh, how civil such a wench is to a man that does her
the honor to marry her.

ANGELLICA.

By heaven, there's no faith in anything he says.   380

Enter Sebastian.

SEBASTIAN.

Madam, Don Antonio—

ANGELLICA.

Come hither.

HELLENA [*aside*].

Ha! Antonio! He may be coming hither, and he'll certainly
discover me. I'll therefore retire without a ceremony.

Exit Hellena.

ANGELLICA.

I'll see him. Get my coach ready.   385

377. has wit] *Q1–3, A;* Whas it *B.*

SEBASTIAN.

    It waits you, madam.

WILLMORE [*aside*].

    This is lucky. —What, madam, now I may be gone and
leave you to the enjoyment of my rival?

ANGELLICA.

    Dull man, that canst not see how ill, how poor,
    That false dissimulation looks. Be gone,   390
    And never let me see thy cozening face again,
    Lest I relapse and kill thee.

WILLMORE.

    Yes, you can spare me now. Farewell, till you're in better
humor. —[*Aside.*] I'm glad of this release. Now for my
gipsy: 395
    For though to worse we change, yet still we find
    New joys, new charms, in a new miss that's kind.

                                         Exit Willmore.

ANGELLICA.

    He's gone, and in this ague of my soul
    The shivering fit returns.
    Oh, with what willing haste he took his leave,   400
    As if the longed-for minute were arrived
    Of some blest assignation.
    In vain I have consulted all my charms,
    In vain this beauty prized, in vain believed
    My eyes could kindle any lasting fires;   405
    I had forgot my name, my infamy,
    And the reproach that honor lays on those
    That dare pretend a sober passion here.
    Nice reputation, though it leave behind
    More virtues than inhabit where that dwells,   410
    Yet that once gone, those virtues shine no more.
    Then since I am not fit to be beloved,
    I am resolved to think on a revenge
    On him that soothed me thus to my undoing.   *Exeunt.*

---

387. may] *Q1, Q3, A, B;* my *Q2.*   414. S.D. *Exeunt.*] *Q1–2, A, B;*
                                                  Exit. Q3.

---

    409. *Nice*] scrupulous.
    414. *soothed*] flattered.

[IV.iii]   *A street.*
Enter Florinda *and* Valeria *in habits different from what they have been seen in.*

FLORINDA.
    We're happily escaped, and yet I tremble still.
VALERIA.
    A lover, and fear? Why, I am but half an one, and yet I
have courage for any attempt. Would Hellena were here: I
would fain have had her as deep in this mischief as we;
she'll fare but ill else, I doubt.   5
FLORINDA.
    She pretended a visit to the Augustine nuns; but I believe
some other design carried her out; pray heaven we light on
her. Prithee, what didst do with Callis?
VALERIA.
    When I saw no reason would do good on her, I followed her
into the wardrobe, and as she was looking for something   10
in a great chest, I toppled her in by the heels, snatched the
key of the apartment where you were confined, locked her
in, and left her bawling for help.
FLORINDA.
    'Tis well you resolve to follow my fortunes, for thou darest
never appear at home again after such an action.   15
VALERIA.
    That's according as the young stranger and I shall agree.
But to our business. I delivered your note to Belvile when I
got out under pretense of going to mass. I found him at his
lodging, and believe me it came seasonably, for never was
man in so desperate a condition. I told him of your resolu- 20
tion of making your escape today if your brother would be
absent long enough to permit you; if not, to die rather than
be Antonio's.

5. fare] *Q1, Q3, B;* fair *Q2, A.*   note *Q2–3, A, B, and some copies of*
7. heaven] *Q1, Q3;* heavens *Q2,*   *Q1.*
A, B.   22. to die] *Q1, Q3;* die *Q2, A, B.*
17. your note] your letter, your

    6. *Augustine nuns*] an order following the rule of St. Augustine.

FLORINDA.

Thou should'st have told him I was confined to my chamber
upon my brother's suspicion that the business on the Molo   25
was a plot laid between him and I.

VALERIA.

I said all this, and told him your brother was now gone to
his devotion; and he resolves to visit every church till he find
him, and not only undeceive him in that, but caress him so
as shall delay his return home.   30

FLORINDA.

Oh heavens! He's here, and Belvile with him, too.

They put on their vizards.

Enter Don Pedro, Belvile, Willmore; Belvile *and* Don Pedro *seeming in
serious discourse.*

VALERIA.

Walk boldly by them, and I'll come at a distance, lest he
suspect us.   *She walks by them and looks back on them.*

WILLMORE.

Ha! A woman, and of excellent mien!

PEDRO.

She throws a kind look back on you.   35

WILLMORE.

Death, 'tis a likely wench, and that kind look shall not be
cast away. I'll follow her.

BELVILE.

Prithee do not.

WILLMORE.

Do not? By heavens, to the antipodies, with such an
invitation.   *She goes out, and* Willmore *follows her.*   40

BELVILE.

'Tis a mad fellow for a wench.

Enter Frederick.

FREDERICK.

Oh, colonel, such news!

24. should'st] *Q1, Q3, B;* should   34. A woman] *Q1, Q3;* Woman
Q2, A.   *Q2, A, B.*
33. suspect] *Q1-3, B;* suspects *A.*

---

39. *antipodies*] antipodes; opposite points on the earth.

BELVILE.

Prithee what?

FREDERICK.

News that will make you laugh in spite of fortune.

BELVILE.

What, Blunt has had some damned trick put upon him?   45
Cheated, banged, or clapped?

FREDERICK.

Cheated, sir, rarely cheated of all but his shirt and drawers;
the unconscionable whore too turned him out before con-
summation, so that, traversing the streets at midnight, the
watch found him in this *fresco* and conducted him home. By   50
heaven, 'tis such a sight, and yet I durst as well been hanged
as laughed at him or pity him: he beats all that do but ask
him a question, and is in such an humor.

PEDRO.

Who is't has met with this ill usage, sir?

BELVILE.

A friend of ours whom you must see for mirth's sake. —   55
(*Aside.*) I'll employ him to give Florinda time for an
escape.

PEDRO.

What is he?

BELVILE.

A young countryman of ours, one that has been educated at
so plentiful a rate he yet ne'er knew the want of money; and   60
'twill be a great jest to see how simply he'll look without it.
For my part, I'll lend him none: and the rogue know not
how to put on a borrowing face and ask first, I'll let him see
how good 'tis to play our parts whilst I play his. Prithee,
Fred, do you go home and keep him in that posture till we   65
come.   *Exeunt.*

Enter Florinda *from the farther end of the scene, looking behind her.*

FLORINDA.

I am followed still. Ha! My brother too advancing this
way! Good heavens defend me from being seen by him!

She goes off.

52. he] *Q1–2, A, B; om. Q3.*   62. know] *Q1; knows Q2–3, A, B.*
62. the] *Q1–3, A; om. B.*

---

46. *clapped*] infected with gonorrhea.

Enter Willmore, *and after him* Valeria, *at a little distance.*

WILLMORE.

Ah, there she sails! She looks back as she were willing to be
boarded; I'll warrant her prize.   70

He goes out, Valeria *following.*

Enter Hellena, *just as he goes out, with a page.*

HELLENA.

Ha, is not that my captain that has a woman in chase? 'Tis
not Angellica. —Boy, follow those people at a distance, and
bring me an account where they go in.   *Exit page.*
—I'll find his haunts, and plague him everywhere. Ha! My
brother!   75

Belvile, Willmore, Pedro *cross the stage;* Hellena *runs off.*

[IV.iv]   *Scene changes to another street. Enter* Florinda.

FLORINDA.

What shall I do? My brother now pursues me. Will no kind
power protect me from his tyranny? Ha! Here's a door
open; I'll venture in, since nothing can be worse than to
fall into his hands. My life and honor are at stake, and my
necessity has no choice.   *She goes in.*   5

Enter Valeria, *and* Hellena's *Page peeping after Florinda.*

PAGE.

Here she went in; I shall remember this house.   *Exit boy.*

VALERIA.

This is Belvile's lodging; she's gone in as readily as if she
knew it. Ha! Here's that mad fellow again; I dare not venture in. I'll watch my opportunity.   *Goes aside.*

Enter Willmore, *gazing about him.*

WILLMORE.

I have lost her hereabouts. Pox on't, she must not 'scape me   10
so.   *Goes out.*

6. S.D. *boy*] Q*1-2, A, B; om.* Q*3.*

_____

70. *warrant her prize*] believe her legitimate prey.

[IV.v]

Scene changes to Blunt's *chamber, discovers him sitting on a couch in his shirt and drawers, reading.*

BLUNT.

So, now my mind's a little at peace, since I have resolved revenge. A pox on this tailor, though, for not bringing home the clothes I bespoke. And a pox of all poor cavaliers: a man can never keep a spare suit for 'em, and I shall have these rogues come in and find me naked, and then I'm undone.   5
But I'm resolved to arm myself: the rascals shall not insult over me too much. (*Puts on an old rusty sword and buff belt.*)   Now, how like a morris dancer I am equipped! A fine ladylike whore to cheat me thus without affording me a kindness for my money! A pox light on her, I shall   10
never be reconciled to the sex more; she has made me as faithless as a physician, as uncharitable as a churchman, and as ill-natured as a poet. Oh, how I'll use all womankind hereafter! What would I give to have one of 'em within my reach now! Any mortal thing in petticoats, kind fortune,   15
send me, and I'll forgive thy last night's malice. —Here's a cursed book, too—a warning to all young travelers—that can instruct me how to prevent such mischiefs now 'tis too late. Well, 'tis a rare convenient thing to read a little now and then, as well as hawk and hunt.   20

Sits down again and reads.

Enter to him Florinda.

FLORINDA.

This house is haunted, sure: 'tis well furnished, and no living thing inhabits it. Ha! A man! Heavens, how he's attired! Sure 'tis some rope dancer, or fencing master. I tremble now for fear, and yet I must venture now to speak to him. —Sir, if I may not interrupt your meditations—   25

He starts up and gazes.

BLUNT.

Ha, what's here? Are my wishes granted? And is not that a she creature? 'Adsheartlikins, 'tis. —What wretched thing art thou, ha?

25.1. *He*] *Q3, A, B; She Q1–2.*

---

8. *morris dancer*] i.e., fantastically attired.

FLORINDA.

Charitable sir, you've told yourself already what I am:
a very wretched maid, forced by a strange unlucky accident   30
to seek a safety here, and must be ruined if you do not grant
it.

BLUNT.

Ruined! Is there any ruin so inevitable as that which now
threatens thee? Dost thou know, miserable woman, into
what den of mischiefs thou art fallen; what abyss of con-   35
fusion, ha? Dost not see something in my looks that frights
thy guilty soul, and makes thee wish to change that shape
of woman for any humble animal, or devil? For those were
safer for thee, and less mischievous.

FLORINDA.

Alas, what mean you, sir? I must confess, your looks have   40
something in 'em makes me fear, but I beseech you, as you
seem a gentleman, pity a harmless virgin that takes your
house for sanctuary.

BLUNT.

Talk on, talk on; and weep, too, till my faith return. Do,
flatter me out of my senses again. A harmless virgin with a   45
pox; as much one as t'other, 'adsheartlikins. Why, what the
devil, can I not be safe in my house for you, not in my
chamber? Nay, not even being naked too cannot secure me?
This is an impudence greater than has invaded me yet.
Come, no resistance.   *Pulls her rudely.*   50

FLORINDA.

Dare you be so cruel?

BLUNT.

Cruel? 'Adsheartlikins, as a galley slave, or a Spanish
whore. Cruel? Yes, I will kiss and beat thee all over, kiss
and see thee all over; thou shalt lie with me too, not that I
care for the enjoyment, but to let thee see I have ta'en   55
deliberated malice to thee, and will be revenged on one
whore for the sins of another. I will smile and deceive thee;

---

35. abyss] *Q1, Q3;* a biss *Q2;* a
bliss *A, B.*
38. those] *Q1, Q3, A, B;* those who
Q2.

55. ta'en] *B;* tain *Q2, A, and some
copies of Q1;* tame *some copies of Q1;*
taken *Q3.*

flatter thee, and beat thee; embrace thee and rob thee, as
she did me; fawn on thee, and strip thee stark naked; then
hang thee out at my window by the heels, with a paper of 60
scurvy verses fastened to thy breast in praise of damnable
women. Come, come, along.

FLORINDA.

Alas, sir, must I be sacrificed for the crimes of the most infamous of my sex? I never understood the sins you name.

BLUNT.

Do, persuade the fool you love him, or that one of you can 65
be just or honest; tell me I was not an easy coxcomb, or any
strange impossible tale: it will be believed sooner than thy
false showers or protestations. A generation of damned
hypocrites! To flatter my very clothes from my back!
Dissembling witches! Are these the returns you make an 70
honest gentleman that trusts, believes, and loves you?
But if I be not even with you— Come along, or I shall—

Pulls her again.

Enter Frederick.

FREDERICK.

Ha, what's here to do?

BLUNT.

'Adsheartlikins, Fred, I am glad thou art come, to be a
witness of my dire revenge.   75

FREDERICK.

What's this, a person of quality too, who is upon the ramble
to supply the defects of some grave impotent husband?

BLUNT.

No, this has another pretense: some very unfortunate accident brought her hither, to save a life pursued by I know not
who or why, and forced to take sanctuary here at fool's 80
haven. 'Adsheartlikins, to me of all mankind for protection?
Is the ass to be cajoled again, think ye? No, young one, no
prayers or tears shall mitigate my rage; therefore prepare
for both my pleasures of enjoyment and revenge. For I am

72. S.D. *her*] *Q1–2, A; him Q3;*   79. save] *Q1, Q3, A, B;* safe *Q2.*
hers B.   84. pleasures] *Q1–3;* pleasure *A, B.*

resolved to make up my loss here on thy body: I'll take it out   85
in kindness and in beating.

FREDERICK.

Now, mistress of mine, what do you think of this?

FLORINDA.

I think he will not, dares not be so barbarous.

FREDERICK.

Have a care, Blunt, she fetched a deep sigh; she is enam-
oured with thy shirt and drawers. She'll strip thee even of   90
that; there are of her calling such unconscionable baggages
and such dexterous thieves, they'll flea a man and he shall
ne'er miss his skin till he feels the cold. There was a countryman of ours robbed of a row of teeth whilst he was a-sleep-
ing, which the jilt made him buy again when he waked.   95
You see, lady, how little reason we have to trust you.

BLUNT.

'Adsheartlikins, why this is most abominable!

FLORINDA.

Some such devils there may be, but by all that's holy, I am
none such. I entered here to save a life in danger.

BLUNT.

For no goodness, I'll warrant her.   100

FREDERICK.

Faith, damsel, you had e'en confessed the plain truth, for we
are fellows not to be caught twice in the same trap. Look on
that wreck: a tight vessel when he set out of haven, well
trimmed and laden. And see how a female picaroon of this
island of rogues has shattered him, and canst thou hope for 105
any mercy?

BLUNT.

No, no, gentlewoman, come along; 'adsheartlikins, we must
be better acquainted. —We'll both lie with her, and then
let me alone to bang her.

---

91. baggages] Q1–3, B; baggage   100. I'll] Q1–2, A, B; I Q3.
A.   101. confessed] Q1–2; confess Q3,
94–95. a-sleeping] Q1–2, A; sleep-   A, B.
ing Q3, B.

---

92. *flea*] flay.

FREDERICK.

I'm ready to serve you in matters of revenge that has a   110
double pleasure in't.

BLUNT.

Well said. —You hear, little one, how you are condemned
by public vote to the bed within; there's no resisting your
destiny, sweetheart.   *Pulls her.*

FLORINDA.

Stay, sir. I have seen you with Belvile, an English cavalier.   115
For his sake, use me kindly. You know him, sir.

BLUNT.

Belvile? Why yes, sweeting, we do know Belvile, and wish
he were with us now. He's a cormorant at whore and bacon:
he'd have a limb or two of thee, my virgin pullet. But 'tis no
matter; we'll leave him the bones to pick.   120

FLORINDA.

Sir, if you have any esteem for that Belvile, I conjure you to
treat me with more gentleness; he'll thank you for the
justice.

FREDERICK.

Hark'ee, Blunt, I doubt we are mistaken in this matter.

FLORINDA.

Sir, if you find me not worth Belvile's care, use me as you   125
please. And that you may think I merit better treatment
than you threaten, pray take this present.

                              Gives him a ring; he looks on it.

BLUNT.

Hum, a diamond! Why, 'tis a wonderful virtue now that
lies in this ring, a mollifying virtue. 'Adsheartlikins, there's
more persuasive rhetoric in't than all her sex can utter.   130

FREDERICK.

I begin to suspect something, and 'twould anger us vilely to
be trussed up for a rape upon a maid of quality, when we
only believe we ruffle a harlot.

BLUNT.

Thou art a credulous fellow, but 'adsheartlikins, I have no

116. him] *Q1, Q3;* how *Q2, A, B.*   133. we ruffle] *Q1, Q3, A, B;* me
                                                   ruffle *Q2.*

---

118. *cormorant . . . bacon*] man of great sexual appetite.

faith yet. Why, my saint prattled as parlously as this does; 135
she gave me a bracelet, too, a devil on her! But I sent my
man to sell it today for necessaries, and it proved as counter-
feit as her vows of love.

FREDERICK.
However, let it reprieve her till we see Belvile.

BLUNT.
That's hard, yet I will grant it.   140

Enter a Servant.

SERVANT.
Oh, sir, the colonel is just come in with his new friend and
a Spaniard of quality, and talks of having you to dinner
with 'em.

BLUNT.
'Adsheartlikins, I'm undone! I would not see 'em for the
world. Hark'ee, Fred, lock up the wench in your chamber. 145

FREDERICK.
Fear nothing, madam: whate'er he threatens, you are safe
whilst in my hands.   *Exeunt* Frederick *and* Florinda.

BLUNT.
And sirrah, upon your life, say I am not at home, or that I'm
asleep, or—or—anything. Away; I'll prevent their coming
this way.   *Locks the door, and exeunt.* 150

The End of the Fourth Act.

141. come in] *Q1–3;* come *A, B.*   150.1.] *Q1–2; om. Q3, A, B.*
150. S.D. *exeunt*] *Q1–3; exit A, B.*

ACT V

Blunt's chamber.

After a great knocking as at his chamber door, enter Blunt *softly crossing the stage, in his shirt and drawers as before.*

[VOICES] (*call within*).

    Ned! Ned Blunt! Ned Blunt!

BLUNT.

    The rogues are up in arms. 'Adsheartlikins, this villainous Frederick has betrayed me: they have heard of my blessed fortune.

[VOICES] (*and knocking within*).

    Ned Blunt! Ned! Ned!   5

BELVILE [*within*].

    Why, he's dead, sir, without dispute dead; he has not been seen today. Let's break open the door. Here, boy—

BLUNT.

    Ha, break open the door? 'Adsheartlikins, that mad fellow will be as good as his word.

BELVILE [*within*].

    Boy, bring something to force the door.   10

              A great noise within, at the door again.

BLUNT.

    So, now must I speak in my own defense; I'll try what rhetoric will do. —Hold, hold! What do you mean, gentlemen, what do you mean?

BELVILE (*within*).

    Oh, rogue, art alive? Prithee open the door and convince us.   15

BLUNT.

    Yes, I am alive, gentlemen, but at present a little busy.

BELVILE (*within*).

    How, Blunt grown a man of business? Come, come, open and let's see this miracle.

0.1. *chamber*] *Q1–3; room A, B.*   0.3. *stage,*] *Q1, Q3; stage Q2, A, B.*
0.2. *as*] *Q1, Q3; om. Q2, A, B.*   5. S.D. *and knocking*] *Q1–2, A, B;*
0.2. *softly*] *Q1, Q3; softly, Q2, A, B.*   *calling and knocking Q3.*

BLUNT.

No, no, no, no, gentlemen, 'tis no great business. But—I
am—at—my devotion. 'Adsheartlikins, will you not allow a   20
man time to pray?

BELVILE (*within*).

Turned religious? A greater wonder than the first! Therefore open quickly, or we shall unhinge, we shall.

BLUNT [*aside*].

This won't do. —Why hark'ee, colonel, to tell you the truth,
I am about a necessary affair of life: I have a wench with   25
me. You apprehend me? —The devil's in't if they be so
uncivil as to disturb me now.

WILLMORE [*within*].

How, a wench? Nay then, we must enter and partake. No
resistance. Unless it be your lady of quality, and then we'll
keep our distance.   30

BLUNT.

So, the business is out.

WILLMORE [*within*].

Come, come, lend's more hands to the door. Now heave, all
together. (*Breaks open the door.*) So, well done, my boys.

Enter Belvile [*and his* Page], Willmore, Frederick, *and* Pedro. Blunt
*looks simply, they all laugh at him; he lays his hand on his sword, and comes
up to* Willmore.

BLUNT.

Hark'ee, sir, laugh out your laugh quickly, d'ye hear, and
be gone. I shall spoil your sport else, 'adsheartlikins, sir, I   35
shall. The jest has been carried on too long. —(*Aside.*) A
plague upon my tailor!

WILLMORE.

'Sdeath, how the whore has dressed him! Faith, sir, I'm
sorry.

---

19. No, no, no, no] Q*1-2, A, B;*   31. is] Q*1-3, B;* it *A.*
No, no, no Q*3.*   32. lend's] Q*1-3, A;* lend *B.*
26. The] Q*1, Q3, A, B;* They Q*2.*

33.2. *simply*] foolishly.

BLUNT.

> Are you so, sir? Keep't to yourself then, sir, I advise you,   40
> d'ye hear, for I can as little endure your pity as his mirth.
>
> > *Lays his hand on's sword.*

BELVILE.

> Indeed, Willmore, thou wert a little too rough with Ned
> Blunt's mistress. Call a person of quality whore, and one so
> young, so handsome, and so eloquent? Ha, ha, he.

BLUNT.

> Hark'ee, sir, you know me, and know I can be angry. Have   45
> a care, for 'adsheartlikins, I can fight, too, I can, sir. Do you
> mark me? No more.

BELVILE.

> Why so peevish, good Ned? Some disappointments, I'll
> warrant. What, did the jealous count, her husband, return
> just in the nick?   50

BLUNT.

> Or the devil, sir.   (*They laugh.*)   D'ye laugh? Look ye settle
> me a good sober countenance, and that quickly, too, or you
> shall know Ned Blunt is not—

BELVILE.

> Not everybody, we know that.

BLUNT.

> Not an ass to be laughed at, sir.   55

WILLMORE.

> Unconscionable sinner! To bring a lover so near his happi-
> ness—a vigorous passionate lover—and then not only cheat
> him of his movables, but his very desires, too.

BELVILE.

> Ah, sir, a mistress is a trifle with Blunt; he'll have a dozen
> the next time he looks abroad. His eyes have charms not to   60
> be resisted; there needs no more than to expose that taking
> person to the view of the fair, and he leads 'em all in
> triumph.

PEDRO.

> Sir, though I'm a stranger to you, I am ashamed at the
> rudeness of my nation; and could you learn who did it,   65
> would assist you to make an example of 'em.

44. he] *Q1-2, A, B;* ha *Q3.*   58. very] *Q1, Q3; om. Q2, A, B.*

BLUNT.

Why ay, there's one speaks sense now, and handsomely. And
let me tell you, gentlemen, I should not have showed myself
like a jack pudding thus to have made you mirth, but that I
have revenge within my power. For know, I have got into　70
my possession a female, who had better have fallen under
any curse than the ruin I design her. 'Adsheartlikins, she
assaulted me here in my own lodgings, and had doubtless
committed a rape upon me, had not this sword defended me.

FREDERICK.

I know not that, but o' my conscience thou had ravished　75
her, had she not redeemed herself with a ring. Let's see't,
Blunt.　　　　　　　　　　　　　*Blunt shows the ring.*

BELVILE [*aside*].

Ha! The ring I gave Florinda when we exchanged our
vows! —Hark'ee, Blunt—　　　　　*Goes to whisper to him.*

WILLMORE.

No whispering, good colonel, there's a woman in the case.　80
No whispering.

BELVILE [*aside to* Blunt].

Hark'ee, fool, be advised, and conceal both the ring and the
story for your reputation's sake. Do not let people know
what despised cullies we English are; to be cheated and
abused by one whore, and another rather bribe thee than　85
be kind to thee, is an infamy to our nation.

WILLMORE.

Come, come, where's the wench? We'll see her; let her be
what she will, we'll see her.

PEDRO.

Ay, ay, let us see her. I can soon discover whether she be of
quality, or for your diversion.　　　　　　　　　90

BLUNT.

She's in Fred's custody.

WILLMORE.

Come, come, the key—
　　　　　To Frederick, *who gives him the key; they are going.*

76. had] *Q1-2;* hadst *Q3, A, B.*　　78. exchanged] *Q2-3, A, B;* ex-
　　　　　　　　　　　　　　　　change *Q1.*

69. *jack pudding*] buffoon.

BELVILE [*aside*].

Death, what shall I do? —Stay, gentlemen. —[*Aside.*]   Yet
if I hinder 'em, I shall discover all. —Hold, let's go one at
once. Give me the key.   95

WILLMORE.

Nay, hold there, colonel, I'll go first.

FREDERICK.

Nay, no dispute, Ned and I have the propriety of her.

WILLMORE.

Damn propriety! Then we'll draw cuts.   (Belvile *goes to
whisper* Willmore.)   Nay, no corruption, good colonel.
Come, the longest sword carries her.   100

They all draw, forgetting Don Pedro, *being a Spaniard, had the longest.*

BLUNT.

I yield up my interest to you, gentlemen, and that will be
revenge sufficient.

WILLMORE (*to* Pedro).

The wench is yours. —[*Aside.*]   Pox of his Toledo, I had
forgot that.

FREDERICK.

Come, sir, I'll conduct you to the lady.   105

Exeunt Frederick *and* Pedro.

BELVILE (*aside*).

To hinder him will certainly discover her. —Dost know,
dull beast, what mischief thou hast done?

Willmore *walking up and down, out of humor.*

WILLMORE.

Ay, ay, to trust our fortune to lots! A devil on't, 'twas mad-
ness, that's the truth on't.

BELVILE.

Oh, intolerable sot—   110

Enter Florinda *running, masked,* Pedro *after her;* Willmore *gazing round
her.*

94. let's go one] *Q1-2, A, B;* let   106. her] *Q1-3; om. A, B.*
one go *Q3.*   107.1. Willmore] *Q1-2, A, B; To*
100.1. being] *Q2, A, B; being as Q1,*   Willmore *Q3.*
Q3.

94–95. *one at once*] one at a time.
103. *Toledo*] fine sword blade made at Toledo.

FLORINDA (*aside*).

Good heaven defend me from discovery!

PEDRO.

'Tis but in vain to fly me; you're fallen to my lot.

BELVILE [*aside*].

Sure she's undiscovered yet, but now I fear there is no way
to bring her off.

WILLMORE [*aside*].

Why, what a pox, is not this my woman, the same I followed 115
but now?   Pedro *talking to* Florinda, *who walks up and down.*

PEDRO.

As if I did not know ye, and your business here.

FLORINDA (*aside*).

Good heaven, I fear he does indeed!

PEDRO.

Come, pray be kind; I know you meant to be so when you
entered here, for these are proper gentlemen.   120

WILLMORE.

But sir, perhaps the lady will not be imposed upon: she'll
choose her man.

PEDRO.

I am better bred than not to leave her choice free.

Enter Valeria, *and is surprised at sight of* Don Pedro.

VALERIA (*aside*).

Don Pedro here! There's no avoiding him.

FLORINDA (*aside*).

Valeria! Then I'm undone.   125

VALERIA (*to* Pedro, *running to him*).

Oh, I have found you, sir! The strangest accident—if I had
breath—to tell it.

PEDRO.

Speak! Is Florinda safe? Hellena well?

VALERIA.

Ay, ay, sir. Florinda is safe. —[*Aside.*]   From any fears of
you.   130

PEDRO.

Why, where's Florinda? Speak!

123.1. *at*] *Q1, Q3; at the Q2, A, B.*

VALERIA.

Ay, where indeed, sir; I wish I could inform you. But to
hold you no longer in doubt—

FLORINDA (*aside*).

Oh, what will she say?

VALERIA.

She's fled away in the habit—of one of her pages, sir. But 135
Callis thinks you may retrieve her yet, if you make haste
away. She'll tell you, sir, the rest. —(*Aside.*)   If you can
find her out.

PEDRO.

Dishonorable girl, she has undone my aim. —[*To* Belvile.]
Sir, you see my necessity of leaving you, and I hope you'll 140
pardon it. My sister, I know, will make her flight to you;
and if she do, I shall expect she should be rendered back.

BELVILE.

I shall consult my love and honor, sir.   *Exit* Pedro.

FLORINDA (*to* Valeria).

My dear preserver, let me embrace thee.

WILLMORE.

What the devil's all this?   145

BLUNT.

Mystery, by this light.

VALERIA.

Come, come, make haste and get yourselves married quickly,
for your brother will return again.

BELVILE.

I'm so surprised with fears and joys, so amazed to find you
here in safety, I can scarce persuade my heart into a faith of 150
what I see.

WILLMORE.

Hark'ee, colonel, is this that mistress who has cost you so
many sighs, and me so many quarrels with you?

BELVILE.

It is. —[*To* Florinda.]   Pray give him the honor of your
hand.   155

WILLMORE.

Thus it must be received, then.   (*Kneels and kisses her hand.*)
And with it give your pardon, too.

140. I] *Q2, A, B; om. Q1, Q3.*

FLORINDA.

The friend to Belvile may command me anything.

WILLMORE (*aside*).

Death, would I might; 'tis a surprising beauty.

BELVILE.

Boy, run and fetch a father instantly.   *Exit* Boy. 160

FREDERICK.

So, now do I stand like a dog, and have not a syllable to
plead my own cause with. By this hand, madam, I was
never thoroughly confounded before, nor shall I ever more
dare look up with confidence, till you are pleased to pardon
me.   165

FLORINDA.

Sir, I'll be reconciled to you on one condition: that you'll
follow the example of your friend in marrying a maid that
does not hate you, and whose fortune, I believe, will not be
unwelcome to you.

FREDERICK.

Madam, had I no inclinations that way, I should obey your 170
kind commands.

BELVILE.

Who, Fred marry? He has so few inclinations for womankind that had he been possessed of paradise he might have
continued there to this day, if no crime but love could have
disinherited him.   175

FREDERICK.

Oh, I do not use to boast of my intrigues.

BELVILE.

Boast! Why, thou dost nothing but boast. And I dare swear,
wert thou as innocent from the sin of the grape as thou art
from the apple, thou might'st yet claim that right in Eden
which our first parents lost by too much loving.   180

FREDERICK.

I wish this lady would think me so modest a man.

VALERIA.

She would be sorry then, and not like you half so well. And
I should be loath to break my word with you, which was,
that if your friend and mine agreed, it should be a match

184. agreed] *Q1–3;* are agreed *A,*
B.

between you and I.   *She gives him her hand.* 185
FREDERICK.

Bear witness, colonel, 'tis a bargain.   *Kisses her hand.*
BLUNT (*to* Florinda).

I have a pardon to beg, too; but 'adsheartlikins, I am so out
of countenance that I'm a dog if I can say anything to
purpose.
FLORINDA.

Sir, I heartily forgive you all.   190
BLUNT.

That's nobly said, sweet lady. —Belvile, prithee present her
her ring again, for I find I have not courage to approach her
myself.   *Gives him the ring; he gives it to* Florinda.

Enter Boy.
BOY.

Sir, I have brought the father that you sent for.   [*Exit* Boy.]
BELVILE.

'Tis well. And now, my dear Florinda, let's fly to complete 195
that mighty joy we have so long wished and sighed for.
—Come, Fred, you'll follow?
FREDERICK.

Your example, sir, 'twas ever my ambition in war, and must
be so in love.
WILLMORE.

And must not I see this juggling knot tied?   200
BELVILE.

No, thou shalt do us better service and be our guard, lest
Don Pedro's sudden return interrupt the ceremony.
WILLMORE.

Content; I'll secure this pass.
                    Exeunt Belvile, Florinda, Frederick, *and* Valeria.

Enter Boy.
BOY (*to* Willmore).

Sir, there's a lady without would speak to you.
WILLMORE.

Conduct her in; I dare not quit my post.   205

193. *ring . . . to*] *Q3, A, B; ring he
gives to Q 1–2.*

200. *juggling*] deceiving (of her family).

BOY [*to* Blunt].

    And sir, your tailor waits you in your chamber.

BLUNT.

    Some comfort yet: I shall not dance naked at the wedding.

                                      Exeunt Blunt *and* Boy.

Enter again the Boy, *conducting in* Angellica *in a masking habit and a vizard.* Willmore *runs to her.*

WILLMORE [*aside*].

    This can be none but my pretty gipsy. —Oh, I see you can follow as well as fly. Come, confess thyself the most malicious devil in nature; you think you have done my business with 210 Angellica—

ANGELLICA.

    Stand off, base villain!

        She draws a pistol and holds it to his breast.

WILLMORE.

    Ha, 'tis not she! Who art thou, and what's thy business?

ANGELLICA.

    One thou hast injured, and who comes to kill thee for't.

WILLMORE.

    What the devil canst thou mean?   215

ANGELLICA.

    By all my hopes to kill thee—

    Holds still the pistol to his breast; he going back, she following still.

WILLMORE.

    Prithee, on what acquaintance? For I know thee not.

ANGELLICA.

    Behold this face so lost to thy remembrance,

                         Pulls off her vizard.

    And then call all thy sins about thy soul,

    And let 'em die with thee.   220

WILLMORE.

    Angellica!

ANGELLICA.

    Yes, traitor! Does not thy guilty blood run shivering through

212.1. *it*] *om. Q1–3, A, B.*   222. traitor] *Q2–3, A, B;* tailor *Q1.*

thy veins? Hast thou no horror at this sight, that tells thee
thou hast not long to boast thy shameful conquest?

WILLMORE.

Faith, no, child. My blood keeps its old ebbs and flows still, 225
and that usual heat too, that could oblige thee with a kindness, had I but opportunity.

ANGELLICA.

Devil! Dost wanton with my pain? Have at thy heart!

WILLMORE.

Hold, dear virago! Hold thy hand a little; I am not now at
leisure to be killed. Hold and hear me. —(*Aside.*) Death, I 230
think she's in earnest.

ANGELLICA (*aside, turning from him*).

Oh, if I take not heed, my coward heart will leave me to his
mercy. —What have you, sir, to say? —But should I hear
thee, thoud'st talk away all that is brave about me, and I
have vowed thy death by all that's sacred.   235

Follows him with the pistol to his breast.

WILLMORE.

Why then, there's an end of a proper handsome fellow, that
might 'a lived to have done good service yet. That's all I
can say to't.

ANGELLICA (*pausingly*).

Yet—I would give thee time for—penitence.

WILLMORE.

Faith, child, I thank God I have ever took care to lead a 240
good, sober, hopeful life, and am of a religion that teaches
me to believe I shall depart in peace.

ANGELLICA.

So will the devil! Tell me,
How many poor believing fools thou hast undone?
How many hearts thou hast betrayed to ruin?   245
Yet these are little mischiefs to the ills
Thou'st taught mine to commit: thou'st taught it love.

WILLMORE.

Egad, 'twas shrewdly hurt the while.

237. 'a] Q *1–2, A;* have Q *3, B.*

---

229. *virago*] woman of masculine courage.

ANGELLICA.
> Love, that has robbed it of its unconcern,
> Of all that pride that taught me how to value it.   250
> And in its room
> A mean submissive passion was conveyed,
> That made me humbly bow, which I ne'er did
> To anything but heaven.
> Thou, perjured man, didst this; and with thy oaths,   255
> Which on thy knees thou didst devoutly make,
> Softened my yielding heart, and then I was a slave.
> Yet still had been content to've worn my chains,
> Worn 'em with vanity and joy forever,
> Hadst thou not broke those vows that put them on.   260
> 'Twas then I was undone.
>> *All this while follows him with the pistol to his breast.*

WILLMORE.
> Broke my vows? Why, where hast thou lived? Amongst the
> gods? For I never heard of mortal man that has not broke a
> thousand vows.

ANGELLICA.
> Oh, impudence!   265

WILLMORE.
> Angellica, that beauty has been too long tempting, not to
> have made a thousand lovers languish; who, in the amorous
> fever, no doubt have sworn like me. Did they all die in that
> faith, still adoring? I do not think they did.

ANGELLICA.
> No, faithless man; had I repaid their vows, as I did thine, I   270
> would have killed the ingrateful that had abandoned me.

WILLMORE.
> This old general has quite spoiled thee: nothing makes a
> woman so vain as being flattered. Your old lover ever sup-
> plies the defects of age with intolerable dotage, vast charge,
> and that which you call constancy; and attributing all this to 275
> your own merits, you domineer, and throw your favors in's
> teeth, upbraiding him still with the defects of age, and cuckold
> him as often as he deceives your expectations. But the gay,

261.1. *the*] *Q1–3; a A, B.*   268. fever] *Q3;* favor *Q1–2, A, B.*

young, brisk lover, that brings his equal fires, and can give
you dart for dart, you'll find will be as nice as you sometimes. 280
ANGELLICA.

All this thou'st made me know, for which I hate thee.
Had I remained in innocent security,
I should have thought all men were born my slaves,
And worn my power like lightning in my eyes,
To have destroved at pleasure when offended.   285
But when love held the mirror, the undeceiving glass
Reflected all the weakness of my soul, and made me know
My richest treasure being lost, my honor,
All the remaining spoil could not be worth
The conqueror's care or value.   290
Oh, how I fell, like a long-worshiped idol,
Discovering all the cheat.
Would not the incense and rich sacrifice
Which blind devotion offered at my altars
Have fallen to thee?   295
Why wouldst thou then destroy my fancied power?
WILLMORE.

By heaven, thou'rt brave, and I admire thee strangely.
I wish I were that dull, that constant thing
Which thou wouldst have, and nature never meant me.
I must, like cheerful birds, sing in all groves,   300
And perch on every bough,
Billing the next kind she that flies to meet me;
Yet, after all, could build my nest with thee,
Thither repairing when I'd loved my round,
And still reserve a tributary flame.   305
To gain your credit, I'll pay you back your charity,
And be obliged for nothing but for love.

Offers her a purse of gold.

ANGELLICA.

Oh, that thou wert in earnest!

280. you'll find will be] you'll will   *Luttrell copy of Q 1.*
be *Q 1;* he'll be *Q 2, A, B;* will be   306. you] *Q 1-2, A, B; om. Q 3.*
Q 3. Emendation from MS note in

280. *nice*] fastidious.

–116–

So mean a thought of me
Would turn my rage to scorn, and I should pity thee,   310
And give thee leave to live;
Which for the public safety of our sex,
And my own private injuries, I dare not do.
Prepare—   *Follows still, as before.*
I will no more be tempted with replies.   315

WILLMORE.

Sure—

ANGELLICA.

Another word will damn thee! I've heard thee talk too long.

She follows him with the pistol ready to shoot; he retires, still amazed. Enter
Don Antonio, *his arm in a scarf, and lays hold on the pistol.*

ANTONIO.

Ha! Angellica!

ANGELLICA.

Antonio! What devil brought thee hither?

ANTONIO.

Love and curiosity, seeing your coach at door. Let me 320
disarm you of this unbecoming instrument of death.
(*Takes away the pistol.*)   Amongst the number of your slaves
was there not one worthy the honor to have fought your
quarrel? —[*To* Willmore.]   Who are you, sir, that are so
very wretched to merit death from her?   325

WILLMORE.

One, sir, that could have made a better end of an amorous
quarrel without you, than with you.

ANTONIO.

Sure 'tis some rival. Ha! The very man took down her
picture yesterday; the very same that set on me last night!
Blessed opportunity—   *Offers to shoot him.* 330

ANGELLICA.

Hold, you're mistaken, sir.

ANTONIO.

By heaven, the very same! —Sir, what pretensions have you
to this lady?

317.1–2.] *Q 3; S.D. follows Antonio's*   319. What] *Q 1–3;* What the *A, B.*
speech Q 1–2, A, B.

WILLMORE.

Sir, I do not use to be examined, and am ill at all disputes
but this—   *Draws;* Antonio *offers to shoot.* 335
ANGELICA (*to* Willmore).

Oh, hold! You see he's armed with certain death.
—And you, Antonio, I command you hold,
By all the passion you've so lately vowed me.

    Enter Don Pedro, *sees* Antonio, *and stays.*

PEDRO (*aside*).

Ha! Antonio! And Angellica!

ANTONIO.

When I refuse obedience to your will,   340
May you destroy me with your mortal hate.
By all that's holy, I adore you so,
That even my rival, who has charms enough
To make him fall a victim to my jealousy,
Shall live; nay, and have leave to love on still.   345

PEDRO (*aside*).

What's this I hear?

ANGELLICA (*pointing to* Willmore).

Ah thus, 'twas thus he talked, and I believed.
Antonio, yesterday
I'd not have sold my interest in his heart
For all the sword has won and lost in battle.   350
—But now, to show my utmost of contempt,
I give thee life; which, if thou wouldst preserve,
Live where my eyes may never see thee more.
Live to undo someone whose soul may prove
So bravely constant to revenge my love.   355

   Goes out. Antonio *follows, but* Pedro *pulls him back.*

PEDRO.

Antonio, stay.

ANTONIO.

Don Pedro!

PEDRO.

What coward fear was that prevented thee from meeting me
this morning on the Molo?

ANTONIO.

Meet thee?   360

PEDRO.

Yes, me; I was the man that dared thee to't.

ANTONIO.

Hast thou so often seen me fight in war, to find no better
cause to excuse my absence? I sent my sword and one to do
thee right, finding myself uncapable to use a sword.

PEDRO.

But 'twas Florinda's quarrel that we fought, and you, to 365
show how little you esteemed her, sent me your rival, giving
him your interest. But I have found the cause of this affront,
and when I meet you fit for the dispute, I'll tell you my
resentment.

ANTONIO.

I shall be ready, sir, ere long, to do you reason.   370

                                            Exit Antonio.

PEDRO.

If I could find Florinda, now whilst my anger's high, I think
I should be kind, and give her to Belvile in revenge.

WILLMORE.

Faith, sir, I know not what you would do, but I believe the
priest within has been so kind.

PEDRO.

How? My sister married?   375

WILLMORE.

I hope by this time he is, and bedded too, or he has not my
longings about him.

PEDRO.

Dares he do this? Does he not fear my power?

WILLMORE.

Faith, not at all; if you will go in and thank him for the
favor he has done your sister, so; if not, sir, my power's 380
greater in this house than yours: I have a damned surly crew
here that will keep you till the next tide, and then clap you
on board for prize. My ship lies but a league off the Molo,
and we shall show your donship a damned Tramontana
rover's trick.   385

                     Enter Belvile.

378. this] *Q1-3;* thus *A, B.*   383. for] *Q1, Q3;* my *Q2, A, B.*

---

384. *Tramontana rover*] pirate from north of the Alps.

BELVILE.

This rogue's in some new mischief. Ha! Pedro returned!

PEDRO.

Colonel Belvile, I hear you have married my sister.

BELVILE.

You have heard truth then, sir.

PEDRO.

Have I so? Then, sir, I wish you joy.

BELVILE.

How?   390

PEDRO.

By this embrace I do, and I am glad on't.

BELVILE.

Are you in earnest?

PEDRO.

By our long friendship and my obligations to thee, I am; the
sudden change I'll give you reasons for anon. Come, lead me
to my sister, that she may know I now approve her choice. 395

Exit Belvile *with* Pedro.

Willmore *goes to follow them. Enter* Hellena, *as before in boy's clothes,
and pulls him back.*

WILLMORE.

Ha! My gipsy! Now a thousand blessings on thee for this
kindness. Egad, child, I was e'en in despair of ever seeing
thee again; my friends are all provided for within, each man
his kind woman.

HELLENA.

Ha! I thought they had served me some such trick!   400

WILLMORE.

And I was e'en resolved to go aboard, and condemn myself
to my lone cabin, and the thoughts of thee.

HELLENA.

And could you have left me behind? Would you have been
so ill natured?

WILLMORE.

Why, 'twould have broke my heart, child. But since we are 405
met again, I defy foul weather to part us.

HELLENA.

And would you be a faithful friend now, if a maid should
trust you?

WILLMORE.

For a friend I cannot promise: thou art of a form so excellent, a face and humor too good for cold dull friendship. I 410
am parlously afraid of being in love, child; and you have
not forgotten how severely you have used me?

HELLENA.

That's all one; such usage you must still look for: to find out
all your haunts, to rail at you to all that love you, till I have
made you love only me in your own defense, because nobody 415
else will love you.

WILLMORE.

But hast thou no better quality to recommend thyself by?

HELLENA.

Faith, none, captain. Why, 'twill be the greater charity to
take me for thy mistress. I am a lone child, a kind of orphan
lover; and why I should die a maid, and in a captain's hands 420
too, I do not understand.

WILLMORE.

Egad, I was never clawed away with broadsides from any
female before. Thou hast one virtue I adore—good nature.
I hate a coy demure mistress, she's as troublesome as a colt;
I'll break none. No, give me a mad mistress when mewed, 425
and in flying, one I dare trust upon the wing, that whilst
she's kind will come to the lure.

HELLENA.

Nay, as kind as you will, good captain, whilst it lasts. But
let's lose no time.

WILLMORE.

My time's as precious to me as thine can be. Therefore, dear 430
creature, since we are so well agreed, let's retire to my
chamber; and if ever thou wert treated with such savory
love! Come, my bed's prepared for such a guest all clean
and sweet as thy fair self. I love to steal a dish and a bottle
with a friend, and hate long graces. Come, let's retire and 435
fall to.

416. you] *Q3; om. Q1–2, A, B.*   426. one] *S (Vol. I, p. 100);* on
420. I should] *Q1–3, B;* should I *A.*   *Q1–3, A, B.*
                                          436. to] *B;* too *Q1–3, A.*

426–427. *flying . . . lure*] i.e., one who can be trusted to remain faithful
as long as she is satisfied.

HELLENA.

    'Tis but getting my consent, and the business is soon done.
Let but old gaffer Hymen and his priest say amen to't, and
I dare lay my mother's daughter by as proper a fellow as
your father's son, without fear or blushing.   440

WILLMORE.

    Hold, hold, no bug words, child. Priest and Hymen?
Prithee add a hangman to 'em to make up the consort. No,
no, we'll have no vows but love, child, nor witness but the
lover: the kind deity enjoins naught but love and enjoy.
Hymen and priest wait still upon portion and jointure; love   445
and beauty have their own ceremonies. Marriage is as certain a bane to love as lending money is to friendship. I'll
neither ask nor give a vow, though I could be content to
turn gipsy and become a left-handed bridegroom to have
the pleasure of working that great miracle of making a maid   450
a mother, if you durst venture. 'Tis upse gipsy that, and if
I miss I'll lose my labor.

HELLENA.

    And if you do not lose, what shall I get? A cradle full of
noise and mischief, with a pack of repentance at my back?
Can you teach me to weave incle to pass my time with?   455
'Tis upse gipsy that, too.

WILLMORE.

    I can teach thee to weave a true love's knot better.

HELLENA.

    So can my dog.

WILLMORE.

    Well, I see we are both upon our guards, and I see there's no
way to conquer good nature but by yielding. Here, give me   460
thy hand: one kiss, and I am thine.

HELLENA.

    One kiss! How like my page he speaks! I am resolved you

---

444. enjoins] *A, B;* enjoin *Q1–3.*   449. left-handed] *Q1, Q3;* left-
hand *Q2, A, B.*

---

438. *gaffer*] old man.
441. *bug words*] threatening language.
442. *consort*] company, usually of musicians.
451. *upse*] in the manner of.
455. *incle*] linen tape or braid.

shall have none, for asking such a sneaking sum. He that
will be satisfied with one kiss will never die of that longing.
Good friend single-kiss, is all your talking come to this? A   465
kiss, a caudle! Farewell, captain single-kiss.

Going out; he stays her.

WILLMORE.

Nay, if we part so, let me die like a bird upon a bough, at
the sheriff's charge. By heaven, both the Indies shall not
buy thee from me. I adore thy humor and will marry thee,
and we are so of one humor it must be a bargain. Give me   470
thy hand. (*Kisses her hand.*)   And now let the blind ones,
love and fortune, do their worst.

HELLENA.

Why, god-a-mercy, captain!

WILLMORE.

But hark'ee: the bargain is now made, but is it not fit we
should know each other's names, that when we have reason   475
to curse one another hereafter, and people ask me who 'tis I
give to the devil, I may at least be able to tell what family
you came of?

HELLENA.

Good reason, captain; and where I have cause, as I doubt
not but I shall have plentiful, that I may know at whom to   480
throw my—blessings, I beseech ye your name.

WILLMORE.

I am called Robert the Constant.

HELLENA.

A very fine name! Pray was it your faulkner or butler that
christened you? Do they not use to whistle when they call
you?   485

WILLMORE.

I hope you have a better, that a man may name without
crossing himself—you are so merry with mine.

HELLENA.

I am called Hellena the Inconstant.

Enter Pedro, Belvile, Florinda, Frederick, Valeria.

---

466. *caudle*] warm drink for the sick.
483. *faulkner*] keeper of hawks.

PEDRO.

Ha! Hellena!

FLORINDA.

Hellena! 490

HELLENA.

The very same. Ha! My brother! Now, captain, show your love and courage; stand to your arms and defend me bravely, or I am lost forever.

PEDRO.

What's this I hear? False girl, how came you hither, and what's your business? Speak! *Goes roughly to her.* 495

WILLMORE.

Hold off, sir; you have leave to parley only.

Puts himself between.

HELLENA.

I had e'en as good tell it, as you guess it. Faith, brother, my business is the same with all living creatures of my age: to love and be beloved—and here's the man.

PEDRO.

Perfidious maid, hast thou deceived me too; deceived 500 thyself and heaven?

HELLENA.

'Tis time enough to make my peace with that;
Be you but kind, let me alone with heaven.

PEDRO.

Belvile, I did not expect this false play from you. Was't not enough you'd gain Florinda, which I pardoned, but your 505 lewd friends too must be enriched with the spoils of a noble family?

BELVILE.

Faith, sir, I am as much surprised at this as you can be. Yet, sir, my friends are gentlemen, and ought to be esteemed for their misfortunes, since they have the glory to suffer with 510 the best of men and kings. 'Tis true, he's a rover of fortune, yet a prince aboard his little wooden world.

---

499. be beloved] *Q 1–3;* beloved *A;* be loved *B.*

505. you'd gain] *Q 1–2, A, B;* you gained *Q 3.*

509. be] *Q 1–3, B; om. A.*

PEDRO.

What's this to the maintenance of a woman of her birth and
quality?

WILLMORE.

Faith, sir, I can boast of nothing but a sword which does 515
me right where'er I come, and has defended a worse cause
than a woman's; and since I loved her before I either knew
her birth or name, I must pursue my resolution and marry
her.

PEDRO.

And is all your holy intent of becoming a nun debauched 520
into a desire of man?

HELLENA.

Why, I have considered the matter, brother, and find the
three hundred thousand crowns my uncle left me, and you
cannot keep from me, will be better laid out in love than in
religion, and turn to as good an account. Let most voices 525
carry it: for heaven or the captain?

ALL CRY.

A captain! A captain!

HELLENA.

Look ye, sir, 'tis a clear case.

PEDRO.

Oh, I am mad! —(*Aside.*)   If I refuse, my life's in danger.
—Come, there's one motive induces me. Take her; I shall 530
now be free from fears of her honor. Guard it you now, if
you can; I have been a slave to't long enough.

Gives her to him.

WILLMORE.

Faith, sir, I am of a nation that are of opinion a woman's
honor is not worth guarding when she has a mind to part
with it.   535

HELLENA.

Well said, captain.

PEDRO (*to* Valeria).

This was your plot, mistress, but I hope you have married
one that will revenge my quarrel to you.

523. three] *Q 1-2, A, B;* two *Q 3, to
agree with IV.ii. 185–190.*

VALERIA.

There's no altering destiny, sir.

PEDRO.

Sooner than a woman's will; therefore I forgive you all, and 540
wish you may get my father's pardon as easily, which I fear.

Enter Blunt *dressed in a Spanish habit, looking very ridiculously; his* Man *adjusting his band.*

MAN.

'Tis very well, sir.

BLUNT.

Well, sir! 'Adsheartlikins, I tell you 'tis damnable ill, sir. A
Spanish habit! Good Lord! Could the devil and my tailor
devise no other punishment for me but the mode of a nation 545
I abominate?

BELVILE.

What's the matter, Ned?

BLUNT.

Pray view me round, and judge.   *Turns round.*

BELVILE.

I must confess thou art a kind of an odd figure.

BLUNT.

In a Spanish habit with a vengeance! I had rather be in the 550
Inquisition for Judaism than in this doublet and breeches; a
pillory were an easy collar to this, three handfuls high; and
these shoes, too, are worse than the stocks, with the sole an
inch shorter than my foot. In fine, gentlemen, methinks I
look like a bag of bays stuffed full of fool's flesh.   555

BELVILE.

Methinks 'tis well, and makes thee look e'en cavalier. Come,
sir, settle your face and salute our friends. Lady—

BLUNT (*to* Hellena).

Ha! Sayst thou so, my little rover? Lady, if you be one, give
me leave to kiss your hand, and tell you, 'adsheartlikins, for

556. e'en cavalier] *Q 1–3; en cava-*
lier A, B.

---

551. *doublet*] close-fitting upper garment.
553. *stocks*] pillory.
555. *bag of bays*] porous bag of spices used in cooking.

all I look so, I am your humble servant. A pox of my 560
Spanish habit!   *Music is heard to play.*

WILLMORE.

Hark! What's this?

Enter Boy.

BOY.

Sir, as the custom is, the gay people in masquerade, who
make every man's house their own, are coming up.

*Enter several men and women in masking habits, with music; they put them-
selves in order and dance.*

BLUNT.

'Adsheartlikins, would 'twere lawful to pull off their false 565
faces, that I might see if my doxy were not amongst 'em.

BELVILE (*to the maskers*).

Ladies and gentlemen, since you are come so *a propos*, you
must take a small collation with us.

WILLMORE (*to* Hellena).

Whilst we'll to the good man within, who stays to give us a
cast of his office. Have you no trembling at the near 570
approach?

HELLENA.

No more than you have in an engagement or a tempest.

WILLMORE.

Egad, thou'rt a brave girl, and I admire thy love and
courage.

> *Lead on; no other dangers they can dread,*   575
> *Who venture in the storms o'th' marriage bed.*   *Exeunt.*

THE END

565. off] *Q1–2, A, B; of Q3.*   576.1. THE END] *Q1; om. Q2, A,*
567. S.D. *maskers*] *masqueros Q1–2;* *B; FINIS Q3.*
masquers Q3, A, B.

566. *doxy*] wench, whore.
570. *cast . . . office*] sample of his specialty.

EPILOGUE

The banished cavaliers! A roving blade!
A popish carnival! A masquerade!
The devil's in't if this will please the nation
In these our blessed times of reformation,
When conventickling is so much in fashion.   5
And yet—
That mutinous tribe less factions do beget,
Than your continual differing in wit.
Your judgment's, as your passion's, a disease:
Nor muse nor miss your appetite can please;   10
You're grown as nice as queasy consciences,
Whose each convulsion, when the spirit moves,
Damns everything that maggot disapproves.
   With canting rule you would the stage refine,
And to dull method all our sense confine.   15
With th'insolence of commonwealths you rule,
Where each gay fop and politic grave fool
On monarch wit impose, without control.
As for the last, who seldom sees a play,
Unless it be the old Blackfriars way;   20
Shaking his empty noddle o'er bamboo,
He cries, "Good faith, these plays will never do!
Ah, sir, in my young days, what lofty wit,
What high-strained scenes of fighting there were writ.
These are slight airy toys. But tell me, pray,   25
What has the House of Commons done today?"
Then shows his politics, to let you see
Of state affairs he'll judge as notably
As he can do of wit and poetry.
The younger sparks, who hither do resort,   30
Cry,

---

1. *blade*] gay fellow.
5. *conventickling*] a pun. A conventicle was a nonconformist religious assembly.
7. *That . . . tribe*] the dissenters.
13. *maggot*] the inner light guiding some dissenters.
14. *canting*] hypocritical.
21. *o'er bamboo*] over a cane.

"Pox o' your genteel things! Give us more sport!
Damn me, I'm sure 'twill never please the court."
   Such fops are never pleased, unless the play
Be stuffed with fools as brisk and dull as they.   35
Such might the half-crown spare, and in a glass
At home behold a more accomplished ass.
Where they may set their cravats, wigs, and faces,
And practice all their buffoonry grimaces:
See how this huff becomes, this damny, stare,   40
Which they at home may act because they dare,
But must with prudent caution do elsewhere.
Oh that our Nokes, or Tony Lee, could show
A fop but half so much to th' life as you.

32. genteel] *Q3;* gentile *Q1-2;*
gentle *A, B.*

---

40. *damny*] expletive: damn me.
43. *Nokes . . . Lee*] the best low comedians of the day.

POSTSCRIPT

This play had been sooner in print, but for a report about the town (made by some either very malicious or very ignorant) that 'twas *Thomaso* altered; which made the booksellers fear some trouble from the proprietor of that admirable play, which indeed has wit enough to stock a   5
poet, and is not to be pieced or mended by any but the excellent author himself. That I have stolen some hints from it, may be a proof that I valued it more than to pretend to alter it, had I the dexterity of some poets, who are not more expert in stealing than in the art of concealing, and who even   10
that way outdo the Spartan boys. I might have appropriated all to myself; but I, vainly proud of my judgment, hang out the sign of Angellica (the only stolen object) to give notice where a great part of the wit dwelt; though if the *Play of the Novella* were as well worth remembering as   15
Thomaso, they might (bating the name) have as well said I took it from thence. I will only say the plot and business (not to boast on't) is my own; as for the words and characters, I leave the reader to judge and compare 'em with *Thomaso*, to whom I recommend the great entertainment of   20
reading it. Though had this succeeded ill, I should have had no need of imploring that justice from the critics, who are naturally so kind to any that pretend to usurp their dominion, especially of our sex: they would doubtless have given me the whole honor on't. Therefore I will only say in   25
English what the famous Vergil does in Latin: I make verses, and others have the fame.

FINIS

0.1.] *Postscript present Q1 only.*   *issue and in some copies of the second*
24. especially . . . sex] *om. in first*   *issue.*

---

15. *Play of the Novella*] *The Novella* (1632), by Richard Brome, is a Jacobean comedy of intrigue from which Mrs. Behn borrowed hints for I.ii.318–332, the idea of the balcony scene with suitors below (II.i), and hints for Florinda's desperate letter to Belvile (I.ii).

26–27. *Vergil . . . fame*] The story is told in an interpolation in the Bodleian manuscript of Donatus' life of Vergil. The poet wrote a distich anonymously for which a hack writer took credit. Vergil then produced a quatrain each line of which required completion, and preceded it with *hos ego versiculos feci; tulit alter honorem.* Since only Vergil could complete the quatrain, the true author of the distich became known.

Appendix A

Lineation as Poetry and Prose

The following notes indicate typographical changes from poetry to prose or from prose to poetry made in the copy text, and variations in such lining among the various editions. Mrs. Behn's blank verse is so irregular, and often so close to speech rhythm, that decision as to how some speeches are to be set in a modernized edition is somewhat arbitrary.

[II.ii]
99–105.] poetry Q1–3, A; prose B.
103–104.] one line Q1–3, A; prose B.
109–110.] prose Q1–3, A, B.
[III.i]
170–173.] poetry Q1–3, A; prose B.
[IV.i]
18–21.] poetry Q1–3, A, B.
24–25. Perhaps . . . basely] poetry Q1–3, A, B.
29–67.] poetry Q1–3, A; poetry except ll. 63–65 prose B.
[IV.ii]
28–44.] poetry Q1–3, A, B.
50–64.] poetry Q1–3, A, B.
99–100.] prose Q1–3, A, B; poetry S.
131–134.] poetry Q1–3, A; prose B.
152–153.] poetry Q1–3, A, B.
164–165. But . . . revenged] poetry Q1–3, A, B.
231–232.] poetry Q1–3, A, B.
245–247.] poetry Q1–3, A, B.
265–267.] poetry Q1–3, A; prose B.
280–281.] poetry Q1–3, A, B.
300–304.] poetry Q1–3, A, B.
315–321.] poetry Q1–3, A; poetry except ll. 315–317 (So . . . on't) prose B.
352–353.] poetry Q1–3, A; prose B.

[IV.iv]
1–5.] poetry Q1–3, A, B.
[IV.v]
31–32. and . . . it] poetry Q1–3, A, B.
[V]
222–224.] poetry Q1–3, A, B.
229–242.] poetry Q1–3, A, B.
263–271. For . . . me] poetry Q1–3, A, B.
320–325.] part of speech poetry Q1–3, A, B.
332–333.] poetry Q1–3, A, B.
365–372.] poetry Q1–3, A, B.
393–395.] poetry Q1–3, A, B.
512. yet . . . world] poetry Q1–3, A, B.
570. Have . . . approach] poetry Q1–3, A, B.

Appendix B

Chronology

Dates for literary works are those of first publication except in the case of plays, where date is that of first production. Publication date for plays follows in parentheses.

Approximate years are indicated by *, occurrences in doubt by (?).

Political and Literary Events	*Life and Major Works of Aphra Behn*
1631 Death of Donne. John Dryden born.	
1633 Samuel Pepys born.	
1635 Sir George Etherege born.*	
1640	Aphra Behn born.* Maiden name and place of birth unknown.
1641 William Wycherley born.*	
1642 First Civil War began (ended 1646). Theaters closed by Parliament. Thomas Shadwell born.*	
1648 Second Civil War.	
1649 Execution of Charles I.	
1650 Jeremy Collier born.	
1651 Hobbes' *Leviathan* published.	

1652
First Dutch War began (ended 1654).
Thomas Otway born.

1653
Nathaniel Lee born.*

1656
D'Avenant's *THE SIEGE OF RHODES* performed at Rutland House.

1657
John Dennis born.

1658
Death of Oliver Cromwell.
D'Avenant's *THE CRUELTY OF THE SPANIARDS IN PERU* performed at the Cockpit.

1660
Restoration of Charles II.
Theatrical patents granted to Thomas Killigrew and Sir William D'Avenant, authorizing them to form, respectively, the King's and the Duke of York's Companies.
Pepys began his diary.

1661
Cowley's *THE CUTTER OF COLEMAN STREET*.
D'Avenant's *THE SIEGE OF RHODES* (expanded to two parts).

1662.
Charter granted to the Royal Society.

1663
Dryden's *THE WILD GALLANT*.
Tuke's *THE ADVENTURES OF FIVE HOURS*.

Period of probable residence in Surinam.*

1664
Sir John Vanbrugh born.
Dryden's *THE RIVAL LADIES.*
Dryden and Howard's *THE IN-
DIAN QUEEN.*
Etherege's *THE COMICAL RE-
VENGE.*

Marriage to merchant named Behn?*

1665
Second Dutch War began (ended
1667).
Great Plague.
Dryden's *THE INDIAN EM-
PEROR.*
Orrery's *MUSTAPHA.*

Death of Mr. Behn?*

1666
Fire of London.
Death of James Shirley.

Mrs. Behn in Antwerp as spy for the
crown (July).

1667
Jonathan Swift born.
Milton's *Paradise Lost* published.
Sprat's *The History of the Royal
Society* published.
Dryden's *SECRET LOVE.*

Return to London.*

1668
Death of D'Avenant.
Dryden made Poet Laureate.
Dryden's *An Essay of Dramatic
Poesy* published.
Shadwell's *THE SULLEN
LOVERS.*

1669
Pepys terminated his diary.
Susannah Centlivre born.

1670
William Congreve born.
Dryden's *THE CONQUEST OF
GRANADA,* Part I.

THE FORCED MARRIAGE, a
tragicomedy, produced at LIF in
December (published 1671).

1671
Dorset Garden Theatre (Duke's
Company) opened.
Colley Cibber born.

THE AMOROUS PRINCE, a tragi-
comedy, produced at LIF in
February (published 1671).

Milton's *Paradise Regained* and *Samson Agonistes* published.
Dryden's *THE CONQUEST OF GRANADA*, Part II.
THE REHEARSAL, by the Duke of Buckingham and others.
Wycherley's *LOVE IN A WOOD*.

1672.
Third Dutch War began (ended 1674).
Joseph Addison born.
Richard Steele born.
Dryden's *MARRIAGE À LA MODE*.

1673

THE DUTCH LOVER, a comedy, produced at DG in February (published 1677).

1674
New Drury Lane Theatre (King's Company) opened.
Death of Milton.
Nicholas Rowe born.
Thomas Rymer's *Reflections on Aristotle's Treatise of Poesy* (translation of Rapin) published.

1675
Dryden's *AURENG-ZEBE*.
Wycherley's *THE COUNTRY WIFE*.*

1676
Etherege's *THE MAN OF MODE*.
Otway's *DON CARLOS*.
Shadwell's *THE VIRTUOSO*.
Wycherley's *THE PLAIN DEALER*.

ABDELAZER, a tragedy, produced at DG in July (published 1677).
THE TOWN FOP, a comedy, produced at DG *c.* September (published 1677).

1677
Rymer's *Tragedies of the Last Age Considered* published.
Dryden's *ALL FOR LOVE*.
Lee's *THE RIVAL QUEENS*.

THE ROVER, a comedy, produced at DG in March (published 1677).

1678
Popish Plot.
George Farquhar born.
Bunyan's *Pilgrim's Progress* (Part I)

SIR PATIENT FANCY, a comedy, produced at DG in January (published 1678).

1679
Exclusion Bill introduced.
Death of Thomas Hobbes.
Death of Roger Boyle, Earl of Orrery.
Charles Johnson born.

THE FEIGNED COURTESANS, a comedy, produced at DG *c.* March (published 1679).
THE YOUNG KING, a tragi-comedy, produced at DG *c.* September (published 1683).

1680
Death of Samuel Butler.
Death of John Wilmot, Earl of Rochester.
Dryden's *THE SPANISH FRIAR*.
Lee's *LUCIUS JUNIUS BRUTUS*.
Otway's *THE ORPHAN*.

1681
Charles II dissolved Parliament at Oxford.
Dryden's *Absalom and Achitophel* published.
Tate's adaptation of *KING LEAR*.

THE SECOND PART OF THE ROVER, a comedy, produced at DG *c.* January (published 1681).
THE FALSE COUNT, a comedy-farce, produced at DG in November (published 1682).
THE ROUNDHEADS, a political comedy, produced at DG *c.* December (published 1682).

1682
The King's and the Duke of York's Companies merged into the United Company.
Dryden's *The Medal*, *MacFlecknoe*, and *Religio Laici* published.
Otway's *VENICE PRESERVED*.

THE CITY HEIRESS, a comedy, produced at DG *c.* May (published 1682).

1683
Rye House Plot.
Death of Thomas Killigrew.
Crowne's *CITY POLITIQUES*.

1684

Poems upon Several Occasions published.

1685

Death of Charles II; accession of James II.

Revocation of the Edict of Nantes.

The Duke of Monmouth's Rebellion.

Death of Otway.

John Gay born.

Crowne's *SIR COURTLY NICE.*

Dryden's *ALBION AND ALBANIUS.*

1686

THE LUCKY CHANCE, a comedy, produced at TR in April (published 1687).

1687

Death of the Duke of Buckingham.

Dryden's *The Hind and the Panther* published.

Newton's *Principia* published.

THE EMPEROR OF THE MOON, a comedy-farce, produced at DG in March (published 1687).

1688

The Revolution.

Alexander Pope born.

Shadwell's *THE SQUIRE OF ALSATIA.*

The Fair Jilt, Oronooko, and *Agnes de Castro* (prose fiction) published.

1689

The War of the League of Augsburg began (ended 1697).

Toleration Act.

Shadwell made Poet Laureate.

Dryden's *DON SEBASTIAN.*

Shadwell's *BURY FAIR.*

Death of Aphra Behn, April 16. Burial in Westminster Abbey.

The History of the Nun and *The Lucky Mistake* (prose fiction) published.

THE WIDOW RANTER, a comedy, produced at TR in November (published 1690).

1690

Battle of the Boyne.

Locke's *Two Treatises of Government* and *An Essay Concerning Human Understanding* published.

1691.

Death of Etherege.*

Langbaine's *An Account of the Dramatic Poets* published.

1692
Death of Lee.
Death of Shadwell.
Tate made Poet Laureate.
1693
George Lillo born.*
Rymer's *A Short View of Tragedy*
published.
Congreve's *THE OLD BACHELOR.*
1694
Death of Queen Mary.
Southerne's *THE FATAL MAR-
RIAGE.*
1695
Group of actors led by Thomas
Betterton left Drury Lane and estab-
lished a new company at Lincoln's
Inn Fields.
Congreve's *LOVE FOR LOVE.*
Southerne's *OROONOKO.*
1696
Cibber's *LOVE'S LAST SHIFT.*   *THE YOUNGER BROTHER,* a
Vanbrugh's *THE RELAPSE.*   comedy, produced at TR in Feb-
                                     ruary (published 1696).

1697
Treaty of Ryswick ended the War
of the League of Augsburg.
Charles Macklin born.
Congreve's *THE MOURNING
BRIDE.*
Vanbrugh's *THE PROVOKED
WIFE.*
1698
Collier controversy started with the   *The Adventure of the Black Lady, The
publication of *A Short View of the*   Court of the King of Bantam, The
Immorality and Profaneness of the   Nun, or Perjured Beauty, The Unfor-
English Stage.   tunate Bride, The Unfortunate Happy
                                         Lady,* and *The Wandering Beauty*
                                         (prose fiction) published in an
                                         edition of the *Histories and Novels.*

1699
Farquhar's *THE CONSTANT
COUPLE.*

1700

Death of Dryden.

Blackmore's *Satire against Wit* published.

Congreve's *THE WAY OF THE WORLD*.

The Dumb Virgin and *The Unhappy Mistake* (prose fiction) published.

1701

Act of Settlement.

War of the Spanish Succession began (ended 1713).

Death of James II.

Rowe's *TAMERLANE*.

Steele's *THE FUNERAL*.

1702

Death of William III; accession of Anne.

The Daily Courant began publication.

Cibber's *SHE WOULD AND SHE WOULD NOT*.

1703

Death of Samuel Pepys.

Rowe's *THE FAIR PENITENT*.

1704

Capture of Gibraltar; Battle of Blenheim.

Defoe's *The Review* began publication (1704–1713).

Swift's *A Tale of a Tub* and *The Battle of the Books* published.

Cibber's *THE CARELESS HUSBAND*.

1705

Haymarket Theatre opened.

Steele's *THE TENDER HUSBAND*.

1706

Battle of Ramillies.

Farquhar's *THE RECRUITING OFFICER*.

1707

Union of Scotland and England.

Death of Farquhar.

Henry Fielding born.
Farquhar's *THE BEAUX' STRA-TAGEM*.

1708
Downes' *Roscius Anglicanus* published.

1709
Samuel Johnson born.
Rowe's edition of Shakespeare published.
The Tatler began publication (1709–1711).
Centlivre's *THE BUSY BODY*.

1711
Shaftesbury's *Characteristics* published.
The Spectator began publication (1711–1712).
Pope's *An Essay on Criticism* published.

1713
Treaty of Utrecht ended the War of the Spanish Succession.
Addison's *CATO*.

1714
Death of Anne; accession of George I.
Steele became Governor of Drury Lane.
John Rich assumed management of Lincoln's Inn Fields.
Centlivre's *THE WONDER: A WOMAN KEEPS A SECRET*.
Rowe's *JANE SHORE*.

1715
Jacobite Rebellion.
Death of Tate.
Rowe made Poet Laureate.
Death of Wycherley.

1716
Addison's *THE DRUMMER*.

1717
David Garrick born.
Cibber's *THE NON-JUROR.*
Gay, Pope, and Arbuthnot's
*THREE HOURS AFTER MAR-
RIAGE.*

1718
Death of Rowe.
Centlivre's *A BOLD STROKE
FOR A WIFE.*

1719
Death of Addison.
Defoe's *Robinson Crusoe* published.
Young's *BUSIRIS, KING OF
EGYPT.*

1720
South Sea Bubble.
Samuel Foote born.
Steele suspended from the Gover-
norship of Drury Lane (restored
1721).
Little Theatre in the Haymarket
opened.
Steele's *The Theatre* (periodical)
published.
Hughes' *THE SIEGE OF DAMAS-
CUS.*

1721
Walpole became first Minister.

1722
Steele's *THE CONSCIOUS
LOVERS.*

1723
Death of Susannah Centlivre.
Death of D'Urfey.

1725
Pope's edition of Shakespeare published.

1726
Death of Jeremy Collier.
Death of Vanbrugh.

Law's *Unlawfulness of Stage Enter-
tainments* published.
Swift's *Gulliver's Travels* published.

1727
Death of George I; accession of
George II.
Death of Sir Isaac Newton.
Arthur Murphy born.

1728
Pope's *The Dunciad* (first version)
published.
Cibber's *THE PROVOKED HUS-
BAND* (expansion of Vanbrugh's
fragment *A JOURNEY TO LON-
DON*).
Gay's *THE BEGGAR'S OPERA*.

1729
Goodman's Fields Theatre opened.
Death of Congreve.
Death of Steele.
Edmund Burke born.

1730
Cibber made Poet Laureate.
Oliver Goldsmith born.
Thomson's *The Seasons* published.
Fielding's *THE AUTHOR'S
FARCE*.
Fielding's *TOM THUMB* (revised
as *THE TRAGEDY OF TRAGE-
DIES*, 1731).

1731
Death of Defoe.
Fielding's *THE GRUB-STREET
OPERA*.
Lillo's *THE LONDON MER-
CHANT*.

1732
Covent Garden Theatre opened.
Death of Gay.
George Colman the elder born.
Fielding's *THE COVENT GAR-
DEN TRAGEDY*.

Fielding's *THE MODERN HUS-BAND*.

Charles Johnson's *CAELIA*.

1733

Pope's *An Essay on Man* (Epistles I–III) published (Epistle IV, 1734).

1734

Death of Dennis.

The Prompter began publication (1734–1736).

Theobald's edition of Shakespeare published.

Fielding's *DON QUIXOTE IN ENGLAND*.

1736

Fielding led the "Great Mogul's Company of Comedians" at the Little Theatre in the Haymarket (1736–1737).

Fielding's *PASQUIN*.

Lillo's *FATAL CURIOSITY*.

1737

The Stage Licensing Act.

Dodsley's *THE KING AND THE MILLER OF MANSFIELD*.

Fielding's *THE HISTORICAL REGISTER FOR 1736*.

CPSIA information can be obtained
at www.ICGtesting.com
Printed in the USA
LVHW02s0825130618
580475LV00015B/357/P